"If you're looking to save time while also crafting food that is healthy, flavorful, and creative, look no further than this essential resource. With *Vegan Pressure Cooking*, JL Fields has crafted that rarest of things: a cookbook that is beautiful and practical at once. The recipes are highly accessible and easy to prepare, and you'll be immediately drawn in by her personable voice and culinary savvy."
—Gena Hamshaw, C.C.N., author of *Choosing Raw*

"A collection of thrillingly easy-to-make, yet scrumptious, recipes that get you to be best buddies with a pressure cooker. JL takes the fear out of cooking under pressure and puts fun and finesse into humble beans, grains, and veggies, turning them into everything from delectable one-pot dishes to desserts."
—Miyoko Schinner, author of *Artisan Vegan Cheese*, and others
(www.artisanveganlife.com)

"In this beautiful and accessible book, the irrepressible JL Fields reinvents 'fast' food healthfully, deliciously, and passionately. And she proves beyond a doubt that this is not your grandma's pressure cooking."
—Victoria Moran, author of *Main Street Vegan* and director of Main Street Vegan Academy
(www.mainstreetvegan.net)

"*Vegan Pressure Cooking* is full of creative, kind, and delicious recipes that'll inspire you to get back into the kitchen tonight!"
—Annie Shannon, co-author of *Betty Goes Vegan*

VEGAN
PRESSURE COOKING
REVISED AND EXPANDED

MORE THAN 100 DELICIOUS GRAIN, BEAN, *and* ONE-POT RECIPES USING A TRADITIONAL OR ELECTRIC PRESSURE COOKER OR INSTANT POT®

JL FIELDS

FAIR WINDS

© 2015, 2018 Quarto Publishing Group USA Inc.

This edition published in 2018.
First Published in 2015 by Fair Winds Press,
an imprint of The Quarto Group,
100 Cummings Center, Suite 265-D,
Beverly, MA 01915, USA.
T (978) 282-9590 F (978) 283-2742
QuartoKnows.com

Fair Winds Press titles are also available at discount for retail, wholesale, promotional, and bulk purchase. For details, contact the Special Sales Manager by email at specialsales@quarto.com or by mail at The Quarto Group, Attn: Special Sales Manager, 100 Cummings Center, Suite 265-D, Beverly, MA 01915, USA.

ISBN: 978-1-63159-421-2

Digital edition published in 2018

Originally found under the following Library of Congress Cataloging-in-Publication Data

Fields, JL
  Vegan pressure cooking : delicious beans, grains, and one-pot meals
in minutes / JL Fields.
     pages cm
   ISBN 978-1-59233-644-9 (paperback)
   1. Vegan cooking. 2. Pressure cooking. 3. One-dish meals. I. Title.
   TX837.F445 2015
   641.5'636--dc23

                                     2014041232

Design: Amanda Richmond
Cover Design: Megan Jones
Photography: Kate Lewis Photography

To Janice and Larry Fields,
for instilling in me a desire to try
to make life better for every living being.

To Dave Burgess,
for loving me for who I was,
who I am, and who I will be.

This book is because of you three.

Contents

Introduction 8

Chapter One 10
PRESSURE COOKING 101

Chapter Two 21
BEANS AND GRAINS

Chapter Three 62
SOUPS AND STEWS

Chapter Four 103
ONE-POT MEALS

Chapter Five 131
MEAL HELPERS AND VEGGIE SIDES

Chapter Six 178
SAUCES AND DIPS

Chapter Seven 191
SWEET TREATS

Resources 202
Acknowledgments 203
About the Author 204
About the Photographer 204
Index 205

Introduction

I hold three people responsible for my pressure-cooking obsession—authors Gena Hamshaw, Lorna Sass, and Jill Nussinow. Four years ago, after eight years as a vegetarian, I went vegan. During that first year as a new vegan, I made a point to read vegan blogs, plant-based cookbooks, and nutrition books. I wanted to get it right, this vegan thing, and after years of counting on my husband to do most of the cooking, I felt like a fish out of water. So when one of my favorite bloggers, Gena Hamshaw of *Choosing Raw*, wrote a compelling, convincing post about the virtues of the pressure cooker—especially for vegans—I was sold. I ordered my first pressure cooker and the cookbook *Great Vegetarian Cooking Under Pressure* by Lorna Sass, and my obsession began.

Not long after learning how to use my pressure cooker, I began to chronicle my adventures (and misadventures) on my blog, JL Goes Vegan. Cookbook author Jill Nussinow reached out to help me along the way. She even wrote a terrific "Pressure Cooker 101" post for my blog, and I began turning to her books religiously. To this day, Jill and I are comrades in pressure cooker activism in and out of the vegan community.

I am not a trained chef. I am a home cook. I simply took the initiative to sign up for a few public education courses at culinary schools to learn how to get more creative in the kitchen and cook intuitively. My recipes are wholesome and delicious and have been developed to demonstrate how easy it is to cook and eat a well-balanced plant-based diet, even if you consider yourself a busy non-cook—actually, *especially* if you consider yourself a busy non-cook.

As a vegan lifestyle coach and educator, I work primarily with clients who are not necessarily inclined to go vegan but are highly motivated to live more healthfully by eating a whole-foods, plant-based diet. I realize that not everyone reading this book is vegan or plans to go vegan. Many people want to learn how to incorporate more plants into their diet to improve their health or to have a more positive impact on the environment. And, of course, there are vegans who want to avoid using or consuming animals. Wherever you are on the veg-spectrum, I want to help. I teach cooking classes and demonstrate how accessible—and essential—the pressure cooker is when following a plant-based diet. I believe that using a pressure cooker will get you back into your kitchen. You will get excited about making dried beans from scratch and getting creative with grains the likes of which you may have never considered cooking or eating.

In this book I will provide you with tips, tricks, and techniques—and delicious, easy recipes—that will help you use the pressure cooker to incorporate more vegetables, legumes and beans, and grains into your diet quickly and easily. Who's ready to have some fun?

CHAPTER ONE

Pressure Cooking 101

Why use a pressure cooker? Simply put, this nifty, no-frills appliance helps you make beans and grains—and, in turn, *meals*—in minutes. Sure, you can buy canned beans or instant rice, but once you realize how quickly you can prepare home-cooked beans and grains, I don't think you'll want to. How *quickly*, you ask?

- Quinoa: 1 minute
- Bulgur: 5 minutes
- Black-eyed peas: 6 minutes
- Brown lentils: 8 minutes

- Adzuki beans: 9 minutes
- Chickpeas: 15 minutes
- Pearl barley: 18 minutes
- Brown rice: 22 minutes

You can also save money. In a cost-per-serving analysis of dried beans versus canned beans, you save roughly twice as much by purchasing dried and cooking them on your own. And you save a lot of sodium too, as the canned versions are often full of salt!

Aside from staples, the pressure cooker is, of course, great for one-pot meals: stews, soups, and more—as this book will show you! For an easy, healthy, filling dinner, I heat onions and garlic in a little olive oil in the pressure cooker and then mix and match vegetables and beans. Another quick and filling meal I love is based around cubed or small potatoes, which cook up in about 6 minutes in the pressure cooker. I cook the potatoes with packaged seitan or tofu, carrots and celery, maybe a diced tomato or two, and enough vegetable broth to cover everything. Six minutes under pressure and I am enjoying a hearty stew alongside a raw salad or sautéed greens.

Now that we know how a pressure cooker can save you time and money—and help you prepare healthy, nutritious, plant-based meals—let's talk about how easy it is to use a pressure cooker. Most people avoid using a pressure cooker because they are afraid of it or it feels too complicated, so let's get all of those pesky fears, apprehensions, and questions out of the way, shall we? I've taken your questions head-on and I've included an entire section on how to use the Instant Pot and other multicookers (page 15). Let's get started!

"I most of all want to thank you for introducing me to a form of cooking that previously was totally intimidating to me. When I tell people I am pressure cooking I get the same response from each one of them: 'My mother had one but I'm too afraid of it.' And my answer to them is always the same: 'If I can do it, you can do it!' My pressure cooker is now a permanent fixture on my stove top, and I plan on happily using it carefree for many years to come."

—Barbara Ravid, recipe tester

Your Common Questions, Answered

One of the reasons people avoid pressure cooking is because it seems alien to them—there are way too many questions and it feels complicated—so they avoid using one. But I assure you, it's just like any other appliance—and once I've answered your questions, you'll be ready to roll!

||||||||||||||||||||||||||||||||||||||||||||||||||||||||||||||||||||||||||||||||||||||||||||||||||||||||||||||||||||||||||||

HOW DO PRESSURE COOKERS WORK?

When cooking traditionally on the stove top, heat rises to 212°F (100°C) and liquid evaporates. When pressure cooking, you lock the lid in place, bring the liquid to a boil, and the heat rises to 250°F (121°C) while retaining all of the steam that would have normally evaporated—this allows for quicker cooking times as well as keeping all those good flavors in, instead of letting them out.

HOW CAN I AVOID BLOWING UP MY PRESSURE COOKER?

I teach pressure cooking classes and this is almost everyone's fear—"the thing's going to blow!" This is highly unlikely, especially these days, with modern-day cookers carrying enough safety features in place to prevent this from happening altogether. That said, be sure to read the owner's manual for the specific safety precautions to follow for your device. In general, these include checking the vent pipe, cover lock, and seal for proper functioning and avoiding filling the pressure cooker beyond the "maximum" line. Some models also advise against using certain foods that may foam or shed loose skin during cooking (such as apples or beans), which can block the steam and release valves, but again, check your model. Probably most important is just staying close to the kitchen when pressure cooking so that you can keep an eye on it.

WHAT COOKS BEST IN A PRESSURE COOKER? ARE THERE FOODS I SHOULD AVOID?

Beans and grains cook up beautifully, and quickly, in the pressure cooker. I tend to cook soups, stews, and vegetables in one-pot meals, but they can be tasty solo, too (though I avoid cooking vegetables alone in an *electric* pressure cooker because they tend to come out overdone). Vegetables don't necessarily cook faster in the pressure cooker, but the flavor can't be beat. Root vegetables in particular, such as potatoes, can cook up in 5 minutes and are always a favorite.

IS OIL REQUIRED TO PRESSURE COOK?

There are two points I want to make about using oil. The first is about safety. There was a time when conventional wisdom suggested that all beans must be cooked with oil to avoid foaming and blowing up a pressure cooker. It was about caution, not flavor. With modern-day pressure cookers, there are more safety features to prevent this from happening, but my general word of advice is to use oil—to avoid loose bean skins lodging in the pressure cooker valve—with beans such as fava and soy and even with grains to avoid foaming (more on that in chapter 2). In this book I will be sure to tell you when oil is essential for safety.

My second point about oil is this: fat—such as added oil or vegan butter—does equal flavor, and I use it in many recipes for this purpose. Although this is not a low- or no-fat cookbook, I have made a concerted effort to offer options wherever possible for those of you following |a low- or no-oil diet. The option is simply this: Substitute oil with 2 to 4 tablespoons (30 to 60 ml) water or vegetable broth for the sauté portion of a recipe.

WHAT DOES COOKING AT "HIGH PRESSURE" AND "LOW PRESSURE" MEAN, AND WHEN DO I USE EACH?

In each recipe, you will see the directive "bring to pressure." You do this by turning the stove heat up to a temperature that will bring everything inside to a boil, which usually means medium-high or high heat. Once it has "come to pressure," you will see or hear a steady stream of steam or gentle rocking motion of the pressure regulator. (Your manual will tell you what pressure looks or sounds like on your cooker specifically.) After it has come to pressure, you will reduce the heat to just enough to maintain pressure. In older pressure cooker models, this may mean medium-low heat; modern-day pressure cookers can maintain pressure on low and sometimes even on simmer.

Beans and grains are almost always cooked at "high pressure." To do this, simply heat up your covered pressure cooker on high. Then, once pressure is achieved, reduce the heat low enough to maintain pressure. Quick vegetable and fruit dishes are almost always cooked at "low pressure." Simply bring to pressure, then reduce the heat so that you have a less intense stream of steam or rocking motion of the pressure regulator than at high pressure. Many new models of pressure cookers have high and low settings (often delineated as "1" and "2").

When you see a recipe that states, "bring to pressure," assume high pressure. I only write low when I really want you to cook at low.

For electric pressure cookers and multicookers, set the cooking time recommended in the recipe to high or low pressure. If you have a device that cooks only at high pressure and you're making a low pressure recipe, reduce the cooking time by one or two minutes.

WHAT ARE NATURAL, NORMAL, AND QUICK RELEASE AND HOW DO YOU DO EACH?

Most pressure cooker recipes will tell you how to release pressure. **Natural pressure release** (or NPR, as it may be called) means that you remove the pressure cooker from the burner and leave it alone. The pressure will come down naturally (refer to your pressure cooker manual for what that may look like, such as the yellow button on the Fagor Splendid or the air vent/cover lock on the Presto handle going down). If pressure doesn't come down naturally in 10 minutes, it's fine to do a quick release (see below).

New-generation pressure cookers, and some electric pressure cookers, have a release valve on the lid, which allows for **normal release**. Just open or press the release valve—don't be alarmed by the steam or sound; that's normal. Pressure will release in a few minutes with the same indications as outlined above. I tend to use normal and quick release for vegetables. For **quick release** hold the covered pressure cooker under cold water (be careful that you don't burn your sink with a hot pressure cooker!) and allow the water to run over the lid (but not the regulator) of the pressure cooker. Pressure will go down in a matter of seconds (longer if you have a whole lot of food in there).

WHY DO COOKING TIMES VARY?

Pressure cooking is not an exact science. Let me repeat: *It's not an exact science.*

Expect some trial and error. I typically err on the side of too much liquid and lower cooking times because I can always bring it back up to pressure and/or simmer to doneness, or drain liquid off. Remember, you can keep cooking *undercooked* food, but overcooked is overcooked for good.

WHAT DO I DO IF THE FOOD IS NOT DONE?

As mentioned above, you can always bring it back up to pressure, or simply simmer, uncovered, on the stove until done.

WILL ELEVATION AFFECT COOKING TIMES?

In a word, yes. The cooking times in this book are based on being at sea level. For my fellow higher-altitude cooks, follow this formula to adjust cook times to your altitude: If you're at 3,000 feet (914 m), immediately add 5 percent more cooking time. For each additional 1,000 feet (305 m), add another 5 percent. I live at 6,000-ish feet (1,829 m) in Colorado, so I add 20 percent more cooking time (5 percent for being at 3,000 feet [914 m] + 15 percent for the additional 3,000 feet [914 m] = 20 percent). I typically opt for the end range of cooking time first and then add my 20 percent—so if black bean cooking time is 18 to 25 minutes, I take the 25 minutes and add 20 percent more time, for 30 minutes total. Grains and veggies, however, tend to cook at the same time as at sea level, so there's no need to adjust time for those.

WHAT SIZE PRESSURE COOKER SHOULD I BUY?

Most people do just fine with a 6- or 8-quart (5.7 or 7.6 L) pressure cooker. If you typically feed a family of six or more, you may want to consider a 10-quart (9.5 L) or larger pressure cooker.

WHICH PRESSURE COOKER SHOULD I BUY?

There are three types of pressure cookers used today: first, second, and third generation. First-generation pressure cookers have the "jiggly" pressure regulator on the vent pipe. Second-generation pressure cookers are quieter and have a spring that holds the valve closed until pressure has been achieved. Third-generation pressure cookers are electric. I use all three types and encourage you to choose whichever type fits you best.

Cost-wise, pressure cookers generally range from $40 to $200 (£24 to £118). A solid second-generation pressure cooker is about $70 to $80 (£41 to £47). It's a modest investment for a lifetime of quick and easy meals!

HOW DOES AN ELECTRIC PRESSURE COOKER DIFFER FROM A STOVE TOP PRESSURE COOKER?

Many people opt for an electric pressure cooker because of its modern features (auto start/stop and warming settings) and possibly out of fear of a stove top model. In my experience, electric pressure cookers are excellent for vegetable broth, beans, grains, soups, and stews. The automatic timing feature is terrific—there's nothing like setting up breakfast in the cooker before going to bed and waking up to hot porridge!

The downside, in my opinion, is that electric pressure cookers often require a few extra minutes to reach pressure, adding to the overall cooking time. In addition, some do not have a sauté function. That means you must either sauté ingredients on the stove top and then add them to the pressure cooker, or skip it and miss out on all that rich, added flavor. Most of the recipes in this book are written to general pressure cooking. If you have an electric pressure cooker, just set the timer for the cooking time in the recipe. If you have an Instant Pot, check out more details below.

WHAT IS AN INSTANT POT® OR MULTICOOKER AND HOW DO I USE IT?

When I first started pressure cooking, it was with a good, old-fashioned, jiggly, stove top pot. And it was with that very first cooker that I started testing recipes for the first edition of this book. As I began working with my recipe testers, it became clear that electric pressure cooking was becoming the method of choice. I jumped on the bandwagon and added the Instant Pot multicooker to my kitchen.

I tested all my recipes in traditional stove top cookers, electric pressure cookers, and in multicookers made by Instant Pot, Fagor, and GoWISE. So, let's be clear right now: **every single recipe in this book can be used in any type of pressure cooker.**

But the Instant Pot has leaped to a category all its own. It's been featured on morning news shows, is the number one best-selling multicooker on Amazon.com, and has Facebook groups with thousands upon thousands of devoted "pot head" members. The Instant Pot is beyond popular—it's cultlike! For that reason, this revised edition includes twenty new recipes written specifically for the Instant Pot or any other electric pressure cooker or multicooker (No fear, pressure cooking traditionalists, I offer instructions on how to adapt the recipes to stove top cookers below.)

So, what exactly *is* an Instant Pot or multicooker? Simply put, it is one compact countertop device with multiple functions, including pressure cooking, rice cooking, slow cooking and—wait for it—even vegan yogurt-making (if you have the DUO or later generation Instant Pot). Sounds pretty magical, doesn't it? It is.

In addition to the various functions, you can set the device to turn on at a certain time. The Instant Pot also switches to warm at the conclusion of cooking so there's not one single thing you need to do. Yep, you could forget that you're pressure cooking, walk out the door, and return 8 hours later to find your rice or beans on warm. Now, I suggest you stick close to home while cooking but, hey, sometimes we get distracted.

Here are a few things I love about the Instant Pot:

- You can set the device to zero (0) minutes to cook tender vegetables (such as leafy greens or broccolini) without turning them to mush. You can also steam tempeh at zero minutes to take the dense edge off.
- Homemade yogurt! True, this is one thing you can't do in a traditional pressure cooker, but it's so fast and easy to make yogurt. Drop the powder from one probiotic capsule (I like 15 billion flora or higher) or the contents of one packet of vegan culture into a box of soymilk—shake, shake, shake—and then pour into jars to incubate 8 to 10 hours. (I have a bit more detailed method, done two ways, on pages 180 and 196.)
- There's a sauté function, which many traditional electric pressure cookers do not have.
- There are three heat levels: "normal" (default setting), "less" (low heat), and "more" (high heat).
- To pressure cook you simply choose the "manual" function which defaults to high pressure (which is how you'll cook beans and grains) and then reduce or increase the cooking time from the default 30 minutes.

Here are the basics of pressure cooking in the Instant Pot:

- Sauté uncovered on less, normal, or more. Use the "adjust" button to toggle from normal to more to less.

When the sauté function is complete, press the "keep warm/cancel" button to turn the Instant Pot off.

- Cover the pot.
- Move the steam valve to sealing.
- Select the "manual" function. The default is high pressure. Use the "pressure" button to toggle to low.
- Set the cooking time.
- After cooking is complete, release the pressure one of three ways:
  - Natural release: leave the device alone and wait until the float valve drops down.
  - Quick release: move the steam release handle to venting. (You'll do this for vegetables, fruit, and some quicker cooking grains. Do not use this release when you're cooking a large quantity of food.)
  - 10-minutes NPR: leave the device alone for 10 minutes after cooking concludes, and then move the steam release handle to venting. This option is somewhere in between the quick release and natural release.

Keep in mind that these instructions are easily adapted to other multicookers, such as the Fagor LUX or the GoWISE multicooker. When you use the Instant Pot recipes that indicate to select manual, do this:

- For the Fagor LUX multicooker, choose the pressure cooker button for high pressure and press it again for low pressure. Then toggle the cooking time up or down, and select the "start" button.
- For the GoWISE 8-in-1 multicooker, choose the pressure cooker button with the "+" and increase to the desired cooking time. The device will automatically start cooking.

For those of you who want to keep on cooking with your stove top pressure cooker:

- High and low pressure is indicated in each recipe. See previous FAQs for how to maintain.
- When instructions call to "set for XX minutes," you will bring to high or low pressure and *then* begin counting the number of minutes indicated in the recipe.
- Natural release: move the stovetop pressure cooker off the burner. Quick release: hold the pressure cooker under running cold water. Be sure to keep the water away from the steam release.

WHAT DIFFERENCES ARE THERE BETWEEN PRESSURE COOKING ON A GAS OR AN ELECTRIC STOVE?

You have much more control over heat with a gas stove. With an electric stove, it may take more time to reduce pressure. One tactic is to use a second burner at the ideal heat for low pressure and transfer the cooker once pressure is achieved.

Cooking Time Charts

Cooking times can vary by the type of pressure cooker, the location (sea level or high elevation), and even the type of stove. Use these general cooking times as a guide, adjusting as necessary to your conditions.

The cook times are the minutes spent at high pressure (or, maintaining pressure). For vegetables, use a quick release; for beans and grains, use a natural release.

Vegetables

TYPE OF VEGETABLE	COOK TIME (MINUTES)
Asparagus, thick whole	2
Asparagus, thin whole	1 to 1 1/2
Beets, large whole	20
Beets, small whole	1 to 2
Broccoli, chopped, florets or spears	2
Brussels sprouts, whole	4
Carrots, 1/4-inch (6 mm) slices	1
Carrots, 1-inch (2.5 cm) chunks	4
Cauliflower, florets	2 to 3
Corn, kernel	1
Corn on the cob	3
Escarole, coarsely chopped	1 to 2
Kale, coarsely chopped	1 to 2
Okra, small pods	2 to 3
Onions, medium whole	2 to 3
Peas	1
Potatoes, 1-inch (2.5 cm) cubes	5
Potatoes, new whole	5
Potatoes, sweet and yams, 2-inch (5 cm) chunks	6 to 7
Potatoes, sweet and yams, medium whole	10 to 11
Spinach, fresh, coarsely chopped	2
Squash, acorn, halved	7
Squash, butternut, 1-inch (2.5 cm) chunks	4
Squash, summer, zucchini, or yellow, 1/2-inch (1.3 cm) slices	2
Turnips, 1 1/2-inch (3.8 cm) chunks	3
Turnips, small quartered	3

Beans

TYPE OF BEAN	COOK TIME FOR SOAKED BEANS (MINUTES)	COOK TIME FOR UNSOAKED BEANS (MINUTES)
Adzuki	5 to 8	14 to 20
Black	7 to 10	22 to 24
Black-eyed	3 to 5	6 to 8
Cannellini	6 to 8	25 to 30
Chickpea (garbanzo)	10 to 15	35 to 40
Cranberry	7 to 10	20 to 25
Great Northern	7 to 10	25 to 30
Lentils, brown	n/a	8 to 10
Lentils, French (green)	n/a	10 to 12
Lentils, red	n/a	4 to 6
Lima	1 to 3	4 to 7
Navy (pea)	5 to 8	16 to 20
Pinto	4 to 6	22 to 24
Red kidney	5 to 8	20 to 25

Grains

TYPE OF GRAIN	LIQUID PER GRAIN (CUPS/ML)	COOK TIME (MINUTES)
Amaranth	2/470 ml	4 to 8
Barley (pearl)	2/470 ml	18 to 20
Buckwheat	2/470 ml	3
Millet	2/470 ml	10
Oats, rolled	4/940 ml	6
Oats, steel-cut	3/705 ml	5
Polenta, coarse	4/940 ml	8
Quinoa	1½ /352 ml	1
Rice, basmati	1½ /352 ml	4 to 6
Rice, long-grain white	1½ /352 ml	4
Rice, wild	3/705 ml	22 to 28

DOES MY PRESSURE COOKER REQUIRE ANY SPECIAL TYPE OF CARE?

Always make sure the rubber gasket is in place and in good shape before using. When it begins to dry out or become stiff it's time for a new one, which you can most likely order from the manufacturer. Also, clean the vents and valves after every use. The owner's manual will explain how to do this. With a little care, your pressure cooker will last you for years and years!

MORE QUESTIONS?

If there are other questions that come up for you and you can't find the answer throughout this book, ask at the www.veganpressurecooking.com community.

Final Tips and Tricks

1. Pressure cookers retain heat really well and get hot, even before being lidded. During the sauté step in a recipe, for instance, you may find some of your vegetables sticking to the bottom of the pan; keep a cup of water or vegetable broth nearby and just add a tablespoon (15 ml) if that happens.

2. Think intuitively! I love mixing and matching beans, greens, and vegetables. Refer to the cooking charts and combine foods with a similar cooking time. You'll have fun!

3. Size matters: Pay attention to the max line on your pressure cooker and make sure you're using a size-appropriate pressure cooker.

4. Don't salt beans while cooking—only once done. (The only exception to this is when you've soaked them overnight and they are part of a larger recipe, such as chili.) I tend to use alternative sodium sources, such as Herbamare, soy sauce, or sea vegetables, and when cooking beans in bulk (for use in other recipes), I don't salt at all. Instead, I stir lemon or lime juice into the beans before storing in the refrigerator or freezer. This allows me the freedom to add a variety of spices, including salt, when using the beans in other dishes.

5. It's okay to have an oops moment. Do you know how many times I've forgotten an ingredient? If you realize you forgot something early on in the process, before coming to pressure, simply quick release (see page 14) as a precaution, open the lid, add what you need, lock the lid in place, and get things going again. If you realize it even later than that, either skip it or quickly cook it separately and add it at the end.

CHAPTER TWO

Beans and Grains

Beans, greens, and grains, that's all we vegans eat, right? Hey, like that is a bad thing? True, back in the day when the perception was that only hippies were vegan, the plant-based diet seemed to be filled with brown rice, beans, and spinach. Today veganism is growing and the supermarket aisles prove it.

But let's remember something—beans, greens, and grains are delicious, nutritious, and an important part of the vegan diet. If you want to eat a whole-foods diet, these are your trifecta!

Italian Lentils, page 24

Cinnamon-Curried Chickpeas, page 25

Umami Anasazi Beans, page 26

Balsamic Black Beans, page 28

Chili-Style Kidney Beans, page 29

Three Bean Delight, page 30

Dill Long-Grain White Rice, page 33

Brown Rice, page 33

Mushroom Rice, page 34

Spanish Rice, page 36

Mint Chive Brown Rice, page 37

Lemon Green Bean Risotto, page 37

Freekeh, page 40

Basic Quinoa, page 41

Quinoa Pilaf, page 42

Polenta Broccoli Bowl, page 44

Italian Pearl Barley, page 46

Basic Pearl Barley, page 47

Bulgur Paprika, page 48

Wild Rice with Dried Cherries and Cranberries, page 48

Lentil TVP Taco Meat, page 50

Cheesy Spinach Oats, page 52

Couscous, Oatmeal, and Veggie Porridge, page 53

Brown Rice and Farro Porridge, page 54

Apple Pie Steel-Cut Oats, page 56

Savory Oat Porridge, page 58

Multigrain and TVP Hot Cereal, page 58

Pumpkin Spice Porridge, page 59

Oat, Amaranth, and Carrot Porridge, page 60

Bulk Cooking Beans and Grains

Bulk cooking—making food in large batches—expanded the diversity of food in my diet dramatically. Spending just a few hours in the kitchen resulted in food that I could reheat during the week and freeze to use later. Beans and grains are perfect for bulk cooking because they are a staple in a vegan diet and they store well once cooked. I tend to make two grains and two beans each weekend. I freeze half of each and use the other half for meals over three to four days. (Take note: Beans can turn quickly, so eat them up within three days if storing in the refrigerator.) Using this method, I build up a rotation of beans and grains in the freezer and find that each week—through fresh bulk cooking and thawing previously cooked foods—I am eating at least four kinds of beans and four kinds of grains—and with minimal effort!

Recipes with beans and grains can be found in every chapter of this book. Consider this section your go-to when just want to cook up some simple bean and grain staples. Lacking creativity? Opt for a "hippie bowl"—a plate or bowl layered with cooked grains, then beans, topped with cooked or raw veggies, and served with a nut-based sauce.

Beans Made Simple

Simple fact: I bought my first pressure cooker so that I could make beans in minutes. The mighty legume is a tremendous source of protein in a vegan diet and, frankly, I was tired of buying all of those cans of beans. What keeps most people from making beans from scratch is one thing: time. The pressure cooker removes that obstacle.

Now, to soak or not to soak, that is the question. Many people are drawn to using a pressure cooker to avoid soaking beans (I was), but soaking does have a purpose: It makes beans more digestible and, even in the pressure cooker, they cook more quickly. In my personal experience, they also cook more evenly and, frankly, taste better. If you don't want to soak beans overnight—or you forget to—you can cook unsoaked, dried beans. The cooking time is longer than soaked but still significantly shorter than the conventional stove top method.

When cooking beans you want just the right amount of water. I have seen instructions as diverse as simply covering the beans with water to using 8 cups (2 L) of water. Ultimately, you will find the right ratio for you based on your cooker and your stove, but let's start with the general rule: cover the beans with water, and then add another 1 inch (2.5 cm). More specifically, when I lived at sea level, I used ½ cup (120 ml) of liquid to 1 cup (170 g) of soaked (uncooked) beans (or 1:2 ratio) and 2 cups (470 ml) of liquid to 1 cup (200 g) of unsoaked (dried) beans (or 2:1 ratio). That formula worked very well for me there, but now that I live at 6,000 feet (1.8 km), I use a 3:1 ratio of liquid to beans for unsoaked beans. (I use the same ratio as at sea level for soaked beans.) When in doubt, use too much cooking liquid rather than too little. Let me tell you, I've burned some beans and that is no fun: it stinks and it's wasteful.

Finally, avoid salting beans before they are fully cooked. The skin may break and the beans may not cook evenly.

Italian Lentils

Lentils cook up quickly and are a great staple in the vegan kitchen.

These Italian-flavored lentils are great in a lettuce salad tossed with sundried tomatoes and green olives or added to marinara for a meatier pasta sauce.

1 cup (200 g) dried brown
   lentils, rinsed and drained
   (no need to soak)

1 cup (235 ml) vegetable broth

1 cup (235 ml) water

¹⁄₄ teaspoon garlic powder

¹⁄₂ teaspoon Italian seasoning
   (or a blend of oregano, basil,
   marjoram, and parsley)

Add all the ingredients to the pressure cooker. Stir to combine. Cover and bring to pressure. Cook at high pressure for 8 to 10 minutes. Use a quick release.

Yield: 4 servings

Cinnamon-Curried Chickpeas

I prefer soaking my beans before cooking them in the pressure cooker, but sometimes I want to make a bean on the spur of the moment. This recipe is the best of both worlds because I quick-soak the chickpeas for one hour in baking soda—a culinary trick I learned from television chef Christina Pirello—for a creamier texture. These beans are terrific served over a bed of sautéed greens.

1 cup (200 g) dried chickpeas

1 tablespoon (8 g) baking soda

4 to 5 cups (940 to 1175 ml) water, divided

1 teaspoon extra-virgin olive oil

1 clove garlic, minced

1/4 cup (40 g) diced onion

1/2 teaspoon hot curry powder

1/4 teaspoon ground cinnamon

1 bay leaf

1/2 teaspoon sea salt (optional)

Add the chickpeas, baking soda, and 2 cups (470 ml) of the water to a large bowl and soak for 1 hour. Rinse the chickpeas well and drain.

In an uncovered pressure cooker heat the oil on medium-high heat. Add the garlic and onion and sauté for 3 minutes. Add the curry, cinnamon, and bay leaf and stir well. Stir in the chickpeas and 2 cups (470 ml) of the water.

Cover and bring to pressure. Cook at high pressure for 30 to 35 minutes. Allow for a natural release.

Remove the lid and stir in the sea salt. If the chickpeas are not done, simmer in the uncovered pressure cooker until done, adding more of the remaining 1 cup (235 ml) water, if needed. Remove the bay leaf before serving.

Yield: 4 servings

Recipe Note

You may use 1/4 cup (60 ml) vegetable broth as a substitute for oil.

Umami Anasazi Beans

Brightly colored (maroon and white-flecked) anasazi beans are
often used as a replacement for pinto beans (because they contain less gas-producing properties) and are typically found in Mexican dishes made with ham. The secret vegan ingredient in this dish, however, is *umami*, the Japanese word for "pleasant savory taste," which is considered the fifth taste in the culinary world (along with sweet, sour, bitter, and salty). Umami foods and cooking techniques bring a sense of meatiness to vegan dishes and lend a feeling of satiety. The pseudo-caramelized onions, mushrooms, liquid smoke, and miso all add a savory flavor experience—no ham required!

1 cup (200 g) dried anasazi beans, soaked for 12 hours or overnight

1 tablespoon (15 ml) extra-virgin olive oil

2 cups (320 g) half-moon slices onion

1/2 teaspoon sugar

1/2 cup (35 g) finely diced mushrooms

1/4 teaspoon liquid smoke

1 teaspoon smoked paprika

2 cups (470 ml) vegan beef-style broth

1/4 cup (60 ml) water

2 teaspoons red miso

1 teaspoon tamari (optional)

Rinse and drain the soaked beans.

In an uncovered pressure cooker, heat the olive oil on high. Add the onion and sugar and cook on high for 10 minutes. You don't want to burn the onions, but you do want to caramelize them, so stirring frequently is essential, as is adding water (as necessary) to avoid sticking. After 10 minutes, the onions should be soft and brown. Add the beans, mushrooms, liquid smoke, paprika, broth, and water. Stir to combine.

Cover and bring to pressure. Cook at high pressure for 5 to 7 minutes. Allow for a natural release.

Remove the lid and stir in the miso. For a saltier flavor, add the tamari.

Yield: 4 servings

Recipe Notes

- Serve in a bowl alongside a side of crusty bread to sop up the delicious juice!
- Yellow miso can be substituted but contains less umami.

Balsamic Black Beans

Balsamic vinegar is a versatile pantry item. You might be accustomed to only using it for salads, but it's also lovely for finishing off a pot of beans. The sweet-and-sour flavor makes this a great side dish or as an entrée served over a simply prepared grain, such as quinoa.

1 cup (200 g) dried black beans, soaked for 12 hours or overnight

1 teaspoon extra-virgin olive oil

2 cloves garlic, minced

1 cup (110 g) diced parsnip

½ teaspoon ground coriander

½ teaspoon ground cardamom

2 cups (470 ml) water

2 to 3 tablespoons (30 to 45 ml) balsamic vinegar, divided

½ teaspoon salt (optional)

Rinse and drain the soaked beans.

In an uncovered pressure cooker, heat the oil on medium-high heat. Add the garlic and sauté for a minute or two; you want it soft, but not brown. Add the parsnip, coriander, and cardamom and sauté for 3 to 5 minutes. Add water if needed to keep from sticking. Add the black beans and water. Stir to combine.

Cover and bring to pressure. Cook at high pressure for 4 to 6 minutes. Allow for a natural release.

Remove the lid and stir in 2 tablespoons (30 ml) of the balsamic vinegar. Taste; add the remaining 1 tablespoon (15 ml) vinegar, if desired, and salt to taste.

Yield: 6 servings

Recipe Notes

• When using vegetables in a basic bean dish (not soup) such as this one, you'll want to opt for soaked beans because their reduced cooking time is more closely matched to the vegetable cooking time; vegetables that cook in 5 to 10 minutes are perfect with a soaked bean that cooks in a similar time.

• Try other root vegetables instead of parsnip, such as carrot, celery, potatoes, beets, or turnips.

• Try using a flavored balsamic vinegar, such as fig, if you like.

Chili-Style Kidney Beans

Red kidney beans are great in soups and on salads. Once soaked, they cook up in 5 to 8 minutes. Use traditional chili seasoning and you can add these beans to a quick spicy soup, scatter on a taco salad, or stuff in a baked sweet potato and serve with a dollop of vegan sour cream. You can also use pinto beans instead of kidney beans if you prefer.

1 cup (200 g) dried red kidney beans, soaked for 12 hours or overnight

1 teaspoon chili powder

1 teaspoon red pepper flakes

1 teaspoon onion powder

$\frac{1}{2}$ teaspoon garlic powder

$\frac{1}{2}$ teaspoon ground cumin

2 cups (470 ml) water

Rinse and drain the soaked beans. Place all the ingredients in the pressure cooker, cover, bring to pressure, and cook at high pressure for 5 to 8 minutes. Allow for a natural release.

Yield: 6 servings

Three Bean Delight

This dish, three nutrient-dense beans—pinto, kidney, and adzuki—cooked with a sea vegetable (kombu) and served over brown rice, is a nod to the macrobiotic philosophy that health, longevity, and healing can be obtained through a simple, plant-based diet. Serve as an entrée, surrounded by steamed vegetables and a simple grain side dish.

1 teaspoon extra-virgin olive oil

½ cup (80 g) diced Vidalia or other sweet onion

2 cloves garlic, minced

2 cups (400 g) mixed dried pinto, red kidney, and adzuki beans

1-inch (2.5 cm) strip kombu

4 to 5 cups (940 to 1175 ml) water

½ to 1 teaspoon dulse flakes

In an uncovered pressure cooker, heat the oil on medium heat. Add the onion and garlic and sauté for 3 minutes, or until the onions are translucent. Stir in the beans, kombu, and water.

Cover and bring to pressure. Cook at high pressure for 22 to 25 minutes. Allow for a natural release.

Remove the lid and taste for doneness. If the beans need to be cooked a bit longer, simmer until done. Stir in the dulse flakes.

Yield: 4 to 6 servings

Recipe Notes

• If you want to leave out the oil, substitute ¼ cup (60 ml) water or vegetable broth.

• Kombu and dulse flakes are sea vegetables, often referred to as seaweed. These vegetables, which also include nori, arame, and kelp, play a big role in Japanese cooking. They are usually sold dried and can be added to soups or used to make vegetarian sushi. All add a deep umami flavor to dishes.

• Herbamare, an herb seasoning blended with natural salt, or other natural salt alternatives can be substituted for the sea vegetables.

Grains Made Simple

Grains are often a staple in a vegan diet—they are in mine—because they are high in fiber and contain protein, B vitamins, and zinc. By simply adding grains such as brown rice, oats, and barley, you will boost the nutrient density of any meal and it brings such a great diversity of taste and texture to meals.

In addition to serving as a side dish or as a base to a "hippie bowl" layered with grain, beans, and vegetables, they are excellent in soups and stews and make for a terrific breakfast.

Note that some grains, such as oats, may foam, so be sure to pay attention to the maximum fill line and the precautions outlined by your particular pressure cooker.

Dill Long-Grain White Rice

Dill brings big taste to the simplest of dishes. Quickly sauté green beans in garlic and serve over this rice, topped with almond slivers, for a flavor-packed meal.

1 teaspoon extra-virgin olive oil

3 cloves garlic, minced

1 teaspoon dried dill, plus more for garnish

1 cup (190 g) long-grain white rice

1 1/2 cups (355 ml) water

1 tablespoon (15 ml) lemon juice

1/2 to 1 teaspoon salt

In an uncovered pressure cooker, heat the oil on medium heat. Add the garlic and sauté for 2 minutes, or until softened. Add the dill, rice, and water. Stir to combine.

Cover and bring to pressure. Cook at high pressure for 18 to 25 minutes. Allow for a natural release.

Stir in the lemon juice, add salt to taste, and garnish with extra dill.

Yield: 4 servings

Brown Rice

Brown rice is an essential in my house. I love having it on hand, and in the freezer, because it's great in soups, in a hippie bowl (see page 22), as a simple side, or mixed with beans.

1 cup (190 g) brown rice

1 1/2 cups (355 ml) water or vegetable broth

Place the rice and water in the pressure cooker. Cover and bring to pressure. Cook at high pressure for 18 to 25 minutes. Allow for a natural release.

Yield: 4 servings

Mushroom Rice

Serve this mushroom rice with a lightly seasoned Asian stir-fry or roll it up in a nori sheet with your favorite vegetables for a hearty vegan sushi roll. When selecting mushrooms, shiitake, cremini, or maitake are all nutrient-packed, flavorful choices.

1 teaspoon sesame oil

1 cup (70 g) chopped or sliced mushrooms

1 cup (190 g) long-grain brown rice

1 ½ cups (355 ml) vegetable broth

1 to 2 tablespoons (15 to 30 ml) tamari

In an uncovered pressure cooker, heat the oil on medium heat. Add the mushrooms and sauté for 3 minutes. Add the rice and broth. Stir to combine.

Cover and bring to pressure. Cook at high pressure for 22 minutes. Allow for a natural release.

Remove the lid and stir in the tamari to taste.

Yield: 4 servings

◀Spanish Rice

Spanish rice is a great side

when serving a traditional Mexican meal, but I particularly love it as filling for a taco or in a taco salad.

||||||||||||||||||||||||||||||||||||||||||||||||||||||

1 tablespoon (15 ml) olive oil

2 cloves garlic, minced

1/2 cup (80 g) finely chopped onion

2 cups (380 g) short-grain brown rice

3 cups (705 ml) vegetable broth

1 tablespoon (16 g) tomato paste

1/2 cup (90 g) diced tomato

1/2 teaspoon cumin

1/2 teaspoon paprika

1/4 to 1/2 teaspoon salt

1 teaspoon chili powder (more if you like heat!)

In an uncovered pressure cooker, heat the oil on medium-high. Add the garlic and onion and sauté for 3 minutes, or until the onions are translucent. Add the rice and sauté for about 5 minutes, until the rice browns slightly. Add the broth, tomato paste, diced tomato, and seasonings. Stir to combine.

Cover and bring to pressure. Cook at high pressure for 20 to 22 minutes. Allow for a natural release.

Yield: 8 servings

Mint Chive Brown Rice

I love this rice with a simple,

steamed vegetable. It's also terrific cold, tossed in a salad.

||||||||||||||||||||||||||||||||||||||||||||||||||||||

2 cloves garlic, minced

1/4 cup (24 g) chopped fresh mint, plus more for garnish

1 tablespoon (2 g) chopped dried chives or 1/3 cup (15 g) chopped fresh

1 cup (190 g) short- or long-grain brown rice

1 1/2 cups (355 ml) water or no- or low-sodium vegetable broth

1/2 to 1 teaspoon sea salt

Place the garlic, mint, chives, rice, and water in the pressure cooker. Stir to combine. Cover and bring to pressure. Cook at high pressure for 22 minutes. Allow for a natural release. Add salt to taste. Serve garnished with mint.

Yield: 4 servings

Lemon Green Bean Risotto

Vegan risotto might be one of my favorite fast things to cook. For starters, it seems like an oxymoron. A traditional, long cooking, heavy cream dish done without cream and in a flash? Yep! Nutritional yeast and lemon juice make a light, vegan substitute for the cream, and the pressure cooker brings it together in a flash.

1 teaspoon vegan butter

4 cloves of garlic, minced

1 cup (70 g) chopped mushrooms

1 cup (100 g) chopped fresh green beans

1 cup (125 g) Arborio rice

2 cups (470 ml) vegetable broth

1/4 teaspoon sea salt

2 tablespoons (14 g) nutritional yeast

3 tablespoons (45 ml) lemon juice

Fresh ground pepper

Heat the vegan butter in an uncovered Instant Pot or multicooker using the sauté function (adjust to less heat).

Select off, and then use the sauté function again for normal (medium) heat. Add the garlic, stir, then add the mushrooms and green beans. Sauté for about 3 minutes.

Add the rice, broth, and salt, and stir to combine well. Cover the pot, move the steam release handle to sealing, select the manual function (high pressure), and set for 7 minutes. Once done, allow for a natural release.

Remove the cover, and stir in the nutritional yeast and lemon juice.

Serve with fresh ground black pepper.

Yield: 2 to 4 servings

Freekeh

Freekeh, or young green wheat, is a popular grain in Middle Eastern cooking and has a lovely nutty flavor and chewy texture. Rich in protein, vitamins, and minerals, serve it with curried beans or dal and a leafy green for a complete meal.

1 cup (160 g) freekeh	Combine the freekeh and water in the pressure cooker. Cover and bring to pressure. Cook at high pressure for 6 minutes. Allow for a natural release; if after 10 minutes the pressure has still not come down fully, manually release.
2 1/2 cups (588 ml) water	

Yield: 4 to 6 servings

Basic Quinoa

Quinoa cooks up in one minute in the pressure cooker. You read
that right! One minute at pressure and then allow for a natural release (up to ten minutes).
Make this hearty grain staple—which is actually a seed (and an honorary legume)—and use it in
endless dishes.

1 cup (175 g) quinoa

1 ½ cups (355 ml) water or broth

½ teaspoon sea salt (optional)

Rinse and drain the quinoa. Place all the ingredients in the pressure cooker. Stir to combine.

Cover and bring to pressure. Cook at high pressure for 1 minute. Allow for a natural release; if after 10 minutes the pressure has still not come down fully, manually release. Fluff and serve.

Yield: 4 servings

Recipe Note

My favorite ways to eat quinoa include:

• Tossed in a salad

• As a warm breakfast cereal, drizzled with maple syrup and topped with chopped pecans

• As the base to vegetable or bean soup

• In a "hippie bowl" (see page 22).

Quinoa Pilaf

You can use this basic recipe and mix and match flavors for a variety of pilaf dishes. Simply substitute the parsley and thyme for other flavor profiles. For example, ginger and paprika with curry vegetable broth and chopped cashews make for a tasty Indian-style pilaf.

1 cup (175 g) quinoa

1 teaspoon walnut oil

1/2 cup (80 g) chopped red onion

1 cup (130 g) diced carrot

1 1/2 cups (355 ml) vegetable broth

1/2 teaspoon dried parsley

1/2 teaspoon dried thyme

1/2 teaspoon sea salt

1/4 to 1/2 cup (30 to 60 g) chopped walnuts

Chopped fresh parsley or thyme, for garnish

Rinse and drain the quinoa.

In an uncovered pressure cooker, heat the oil on medium heat. Add the onion and carrot and sauté for 3 minutes. Add the vegetable broth, dried parsley, dried thyme, salt, and quinoa. Stir to combine.

Cover and bring to pressure. Cook at high pressure for 1 minute. Allow for a natural release; if after 10 minutes the pressure has still not come down fully, manually release.

Fluff the quinoa before gently mixing in the walnuts. Serve with a garnish of fresh parsley or thyme.

Yield: 4 servings

Recipe Note

If you don't have walnut oil, substitute vegetable oil or 1/4 cup (60 ml) vegetable broth or water.

Polenta Broccoli Bowl

Polenta might be one of the easiest things you've never made. Sure, you can buy a tube at the store, but once you make this I think you'll see this is an easy staple to add to your meal rotation. To serve this comforting, creamy dish, spoon over steamed broccoli and garnish with fresh herbs or diced tomato (cooked or raw). Note: I recommend that you do not stir the cornmeal into the broth, to keep the polenta from sticking.

4 cups (940 ml) vegetable broth

3 cloves garlic, minced

$\frac{1}{2}$ teaspoon turmeric

$\frac{1}{2}$ teaspoon ground cumin

$\frac{1}{2}$ teaspoon smoked paprika

1 cup (140 g) cornmeal

2 cups (142 g) broccoli florets

$\frac{1}{4}$ cup (24 g) nutritional yeast

2 teaspoons (10 g) vegan butter

2 teaspoons (10 ml) lemon juice

Salt, to taste (optional)

Fresh herbs or diced tomatoes, for garnish

Combine the broth, garlic, turmeric, cumin, and paprika in the uncovered Instant Pot or multicooker. Pour the cornmeal into the pot but *do not* stir (this helps avoid scorching). Cover the pot, select manual (high pressure), and set for 5 minutes. Once done, allow for a natural release.

While the pressure is releasing, steam or sauté the broccoli.

Once pressure is released, remove the cover and whisk the polenta until smooth. Stir in the nutritional yeast, butter, and lemon juice. Taste before adding salt.

Place the steamed broccoli in serving bowls and spoon the polenta over top. Garnish with herbs or tomatoes.

Yield: 4 servings

◀ Italian Pearl Barley

Popular in hearty soups and stews, pearl barley is also used in orzotto, which is similar to risotto. With just a few seasonings, this is a terrific side to any kind of Mediterranean main dish.

‖‖

1 cup (200 g) pearl barley

3 cups (705 ml) vegetable broth

½ teaspoon dried oregano

½ teaspoon dried basil

Add all the ingredients to the pressure cooker. Cover and bring to pressure. Cook at high pressure for 18 to 20 minutes. Use a quick release.

Yield: 4 to 6 servings

Basic Pearl Barley

This adaptable grain can be used in place of brown rice, as an alternative to oatmeal for breakfast, as a hearty addition to a soup or stew, and even in risotto. I add it to Italian-style hippie bowls such as the Mediterranean Beans with Greens on page 172.

‖‖

1 cup (200 g) pearl barley

2 cups (470 ml) water

Add the barley and water to the pressure cooker. Cover and bring to pressure. Cook at high pressure for 18 to 20 minutes. Allow for a natural release.

Yield: 4 servings

Bulgur Paprika

Bulgur wheat is a chewy grain that bulks up soups, stews, and salads. It's also a great replacement for rice. The addition of garlic and paprika (I prefer smoked or Hungarian in this dish) brings an exotic aroma and vibrant color to a very simple side dish—excellent alongside chickpeas or black beans.

||||||||||||||||||||||||||||||||||||||||||||||||||||||

1 teaspoon extra-virgin olive oil

3 cloves garlic, minced

1 tablespoon (7 g) paprika

1 cup (185 g) bulgur

1 teaspoon sea salt

1³/₄ cups (411 ml) water

In an uncovered pressure cooker, heat the olive oil on medium heat. Add the garlic and sauté for no more than 30 seconds. Add the paprika, bulgur, salt, and water. Stir to combine.

Cover and bring to pressure. Cook at high pressure for 5 minutes. Allow for a natural release; if after 10 minutes the pressure has still not come down fully, manually release. Fluff the bulgur gently with a fork.

Yield: 4 to 6 servings

Wild Rice with Dried Cherries and Cranberries ▶

Just right for the holiday table, this is a great side with a vegan roast—or add cooked lentils and let it stand alone as a festive entrée. If you want to skip the oil, add ¹/₄ cup (60 ml) water or vegetable broth.

||||||||||||||||||||||||||||||||||||||||||||||||||||||

1 teaspoon extra-virgin olive oil

¹/₄ cup (25 g) chopped celery

¹/₄ cup (40 g) diced onion

1 cup (160 g) wild rice

1 cup (120 g) mix of dried cranberries and dried cherries

¹/₂ teaspoon dried thyme

¹/₂ teaspoon dried sage

3 to 3¹/₂ cups (705 to 825 ml) water

Salt, to taste

In an uncovered pressure cooker, heat the oil on medium-high. Add the celery and onion and sauté until the celery is soft, 3 to 4 minutes. Add the rice, dried fruit, thyme, sage, and water. Stir to combine.

Cover and bring to pressure. Cook at high pressure for 22 to 25 minutes. Allow for a natural release. Add salt to taste.

Yield: 4 servings

Lentil TVP Taco Meat

TVP, or textured vegetable protein, is a soy-based product that boosts the nutrition level of this dish and will keep you satisfied. This recipe is a solid base for any vegan Mexican dish. Brown it in a hot skillet with garlic and onion for taco meat. Mix it with green chilies and enchilada sauce before filling corn or flour tortillas in enchiladas. Or mix it with raw, chopped, bell and jalapeño peppers, and serve over a plate of leafy greens for a simple taco salad.

1 cup (200 g) dried green or brown lentils

1 cup (100 g) TVP

2 cups (470 ml) beef-style vegan broth or other vegetable broth

1/2 cup (120 ml) water

2 teaspoons (5 g) taco seasoning

1 teaspoon tomato powder (or 2 teaspoons tomato paste)

1/4 teaspoon mesquite liquid smoke

Combine all the ingredients in the Instant Pot or multi-cooker. Cover, move the steam release handle to sealing, select the manual function (high pressure), and set for 10 minutes. Once done, allow for a natural release.

Yield: 6 to 8 servings

Hot Breakfasts
Made Simple

Porridge and hot cereals are my favorite breakfast and a great way to fit more whole grains into your diet. I tend to mix and match grains with similar cooking times and then use a variety of liquids. Water is always an option but sometimes mixing things up with a plant milk, or even a vegetable broth, adds a special creaminess and intensified flavor profile.

If you're using an electric pressure cooker you can easily set up your unit to automatically begin cooking before you wake up—there's nothing better than waking up to a hot breakfast!

Cheesy Spinach Oats

I remain a fan of savory oats. There are so many variations! You can change this one up by adding a couple cups of chopped cauliflower or broccoli—just be sure to add them to the pot to cook with the oats.

1 cup (80 g) chopped onion

1 teaspoon dried oregano

½ teaspoon cumin

½ teaspoon chili powder

½ teaspoon black pepper

3 cups (705 ml) chicken-style vegan broth

1 cup (80 g) steel-cut oats

2 tablespoons (14 g) nutritional yeast

4 cups (260 g) tightly packed baby spinach

Salt, to taste (optional)

Ground black pepper, to taste (optional)

Dry-sauté the onion in the Instant Pot or multicooker for 3 to 5 minutes by selecting the sauté function and adjust to less heat. Add a little water or vegetable broth if the onion begins to stick. Add the oregano, cumin, chili powder, pepper, broth, and steel-cut oats. Combine well. Cover the pot, move the steam release handle to sealing, select manual (high pressure), and set for 5 minutes. Once done, allow for a natural release.

Once pressure has been released, remove the cover and stir in the nutritional yeast and baby spinach. Prop the lid over the pot, without sealing, for just a few minutes to allow the spinach to wilt slightly.

Add salt and pepper, and serve.

Yield: 4 servings

Recipe Notes

• Remember, if you'd like to use a heartier vegetable—such as cauliflower or broccoli— add them to the pot to cook with all of the other ingredients.

• For the broth, I like to use Massel Bouillon and Seasonings USA.

Couscous, Oatmeal, and Veggie Porridge

I love a savory breakfast, and adding vegetables to a traditional oat or porridge dish can do just the trick. For a richer flavor consider using a vegan-beef or chicken-style broth. Toasted nuts or seeds—consider tamari seasoned pumpkin seeds—make for a great garnish, too.

2 tablespoons (28 g) vegan butter

¼ cup (40 g) diced yellow onion

2 cups (260 g) finely, evenly diced carrots

5 cups (1.2 L ml) water

1 cup (175 g) couscous

1 cup (80 g) rolled oats

1 teaspoon sea salt

½ teaspoon cinnamon

In an uncovered pressure cooker heat the vegan butter on medium-high heat. Add the onion and sauté for 1 minute. Add the carrots, and then add the water, couscous, oats, salt, and cinnamon. Stir to combine.

Cover and bring to pressure. Cook at high pressure for 5 minutes. Allow for a natural release; if after 10 minutes the pressure has still not come down fully, manually release. Remove the lid, fluff, and serve.

Yield: 4 servings

Recipe Note

For added creaminess, substitute coconut or almond milk for the water.

Brown Rice and Farro Porridge

Farro has twice the fiber and protein of traditional wheat, making
this a healthy breakfast alternative. Farro has a natural, nutty undertone with a hint of cinnamon,
making it an ideal addition to a savory breakfast dish.

½ cup (95 g) short-grain
  brown rice, rinsed and
  drained

½ cup (90 g) farro, rinsed
  and drained

½ cup (65 g) frozen corn

2 ¼ cups (530 ml) water

Pinch of salt

Fresh basil, for garnish (optional)

Add the rice, farro, corn, water, and salt to the pressure
cooker. Stir to combine.

Cover and bring to pressure. Cook at high pressure for
20 minutes. Allow for a natural release; if after 10 minutes the pressure has still not come down fully, manually
release. Garnish with basil.

Yield: 4 to 6 servings

Apple Pie Steel-Cut Oats

Dessert for breakfast? When it's this nutritious, why not? Well, this isn't exactly dessert, but it is an especially sweet, hot breakfast. Peaches and berries are a great substitute for the apple, as are raisins or dried cranberries for the dates.

1 cup (80 g) steel-cut oats

1 cup (235 ml) almond milk

2 cups (470 ml) water

1 cup (150 g) diced apple

1 large medjool date, chopped

½ teaspoon ground cinnamon

Pinch of sea salt

Add all the ingredients to the pressure cooker. Cover and bring to pressure. Cook at pressure for 3 minutes. Allow for a natural release.

Yield: 4 servings

Recipe Note

Play with the liquid, just keep the ratio intact! Replacing some of the water with almond, soy, or coconut milk makes for a creamy texture.

Savory Oat Porridge

Pumpkin seeds, almonds, and

vegetable broth turn breakfast on its ear with another savory oat option.

IIIIIIIIIIIIIIIIIIIIIIIIIIIIIIIIIIIIIIIIIIIIIIIIIIIIIII

1 cup (80 g) rolled oats (not instant)

1/4 cup (20 g) steel-cut oats

1 tablespoon (8 g) amaranth

1/4 cup (30 g) pepitas (pumpkin seeds), plus more for garnish

1/4 cup (27 g) almond slivers

2 tablespoons (14 g) nutritional yeast flakes

1 1/4 cups (295 ml) low-sodium vegetable broth

1 1/4 cups (295 ml) unflavored flaxseed milk (or other plant-based milk)

Herbamare or sea salt, to taste

Add the rolled oats, steel-cut oats, amaranth, pepitas, almonds, nutritional yeast, broth, and milk to the pressure cooker. Stir to combine.

Cover and bring to pressure and cook at high pressure for 3 minutes. Allow for a normal release.

Add Herbamare to taste and garnish with additional pepitas.

Yield: 4 to 6 servings

Multigrain and TVP Hot Cereal

For a savory cereal, use vegetable

broth instead of water and serve with a salty nut; for a sweeter version, use almond or coconut milk instead of water and top with dried fruit.

IIIIIIIIIIIIIIIIIIIIIIIIIIIIIIIIIIIIIIIIIIIIIIIIIIIIIII

1 cup (100 g) multigrain cereal mix

1/2 cup (50 g) TVP

3 cups (705 ml) water

Add all the ingredients to the pressure cooker. Stir to combine. Cover and bring to pressure. Cook at high pressure for 4 minutes. Allow for a natural release.

Yield: 2 to 3 servings

Pumpkin Spice Porridge

The first time I made this hot breakfast bowl was on a cold Colorado morning, a few days before Thanksgiving. It's now a holiday favorite. If you can't find pumpkin spice coconut milk at the store (it is a seasonal product), just substitute 2 cups (470 ml) regular coconut milk plus 1 tablespoon (6 g) pumpkin pie spice.

½ cup (88 g) quinoa

¼ cup (32 g) amaranth

¼ cup (44 g) couscous

2 cups (470 ml) pumpkin spice coconut milk, such as So Delicious

¼ cup (60 ml) water

Pumpkin seeds, for garnish

Dried cranberries, for garnish

Add the quinoa, amaranth, couscous, coconut milk, and water to the pressure cooker. Stir to combine.

Cover and bring to pressure. Cook at high pressure for 10 minutes. Allow for a natural release.

Garnish with the pumpkin seeds and dried cranberries.

Yield: 4 to 6 servings

Oat, Amaranth, and Carrot Porridge

Similar to the couscous porridge on page 53, this recipe has a decreased cooking time. Consider replacing the carrots with 1 cup (150 g) of vegetables that cook up in about four minutes: cubed butternut squash, cauliflower florets, or cubed fingerling potatoes.

||||||||||||||||||||||||||||||||||||||||||||||||||||||||||||||||||||||||||||||||||||||||||||||||||||||||||||||||||||

2 tablespoons (28 g) vegan butter

¼ cup (40 g) diced yellow onion

2 carrots, diced

1 cup (80 g) rolled oats

1 cup (130 g) amaranth

2½ cups (588 ml) water

1 teaspoon salt

½ teaspoon ground cinnamon

In an uncovered pressure cooker, heat the vegan butter on medium heat. Add the onion and carrots and sauté until the onions are translucent, 3 to 4 minutes. Add the oats, amaranth, water, salt, and cinnamon. Stir to combine.

Cover and bring to pressure. Cook at high pressure for 4 minutes. Allow for a natural release.

Yield: 4 servings

CHAPTER THREE

Soups and Stews

I bought my first pressure cooker to make quick-cooking beans and grains. I fell in love with my pressure cooker when I realized I could also make soups and stews in no time at all—often featuring those beans and grains! Of course, most soups can be made with water, but I find using vegetable broth is a great way to add flavor. If in chapter 2 I convinced you to quit buying canned beans, perhaps the first thing I can do in this chapter is encourage you to start making your own vegetable broth—it's so darn easy! Throughout this book whenever I call for vegetable broth, consider using your very own homemade broth.

Basic Vegetable Broth, page 63

Vegetable Scrap Broth, page 64

Easy Black Bean Soup, page 65

Garam Masala Soup, page 65

White Beans and Greens Soup, page 66

Curried Mung Bean Stew, page 68

Potato Soup, page 70

Creamy Kale Miso Soup, page 72

Chik'n Lentil Noodle Soup, page 74

Portobello Mushroom and Barley Soup, page 76

Very Veggie Split Pea Soup, page 78

Potato, Apple, and Lentil Soup, page 79

Tofu, Chickpea, Artichoke, and Potato Soup, page 80

Bean and Barley Stew, page 81

Vegan "Turkey," Bean, and Kale Soup, page 82

Cream of Asparagus and Potato Soup, page 84

Instant Pot Miso Soup, page 85

Anasazi Bean and Potato Soup, page 86

Speedy Bean Chili, page 87

Black Bean and Sweet Potato Stew, page 88

Kale, Lentil, and Squash Chili, page 90

Flageolet Bean and Millet Stew, page 91

Split Pea and Barley Stew, page 92

Refried Bean and Tempeh Soup (or Stew), page 94

Chunky Red Lentil Stew, page 96

Black-Eyed Pea and Collard Green Chili, page 98

Asian Adzuki Bean Chili, page 100

Summer Lentil and Millet Chili, page 102

Basic Vegetable Broth

Years ago, while interviewing a chef in New York for a piece I was writing for *The Journal News*, he shared this tip with me: Adding fruit—such as peaches, pears, or apples—to vegetable broths brings flavor and also keeps the broth clear. This works particularly well for making broth for "light" or cream soups. My recipe is inspired by that tip!

1 peach, quartered

2 apples, quartered

1 medium onion, quartered

4 cloves garlic, chopped (peel and all)

8 carrots, halved

6 stalks celery, halved

1 tomato, quartered

6 whole romaine lettuce leaves

1 teaspoon avocado oil (optional)

8 cups (2 L) water

½ teaspoon dried oregano

½ teaspoon dried sage

½ teaspoon dried sweet basil

½ teaspoon dried whole (rubbed) rosemary

1 teaspoon sea salt (optional)

Place all the ingredients in the pressure cooker. Stir to combine.

Cover and bring to pressure. Cook at high pressure for 15 to 30 minutes (for a richer broth, opt for 30 minutes).

Remove from the heat and allow for a natural release. Remove the lid from the pressure cooker.

Strain the broth through a fine-mesh strainer or cheesecloth. Use immediately or store in an airtight glass jar or container for up to 1 week; freeze in a heavy-duty freezer bag for 3 to 6 months.

Yield: 6 to 8 cups (1.4 to 2 L)

Vegetable Scrap Broth

While not the most appealing recipe title, this is my go-to method

for making delicious, homemade vegetable broth on a weekly basis. I save vegetable and fruit scraps throughout the week and store them in the freezer in a sturdy plastic bag. This reduces waste and it makes a practical, flavorful vegetable broth to use when cooking soups, grains, and beans, and for reheating bulk-cooked foods.

1 gallon (3.8 L) freezer bag full of vegetable scraps

8 cups (2 L) water

2 bay leaves

½ teaspoon each of 3 or 4 spices of choice

1 teaspoon sea salt (optional)

Thaw (or partially thaw) the frozen vegetable scraps. Rinse well and drain.

Place the vegetables in the pressure cooker and add the water and seasonings. Stir to combine.

Cover and bring to pressure. Cook at high pressure 15 to 30 minutes (for a richer broth, opt for 30 minutes). Allow for a natural release.

Remove the lid from the pressure cooker. Strain the broth through a fine-mesh strainer or cheesecloth.

If not using immediately, store in an airtight glass jar or container for 3 to 5 days, or freeze in a heavy-duty freezer bag for 3 to 6 months.

Yield: 8 cups (2 L)

Recipe Notes

• Some of my favorite scraps include red and yellow onion pieces, including peel; garlic and skin; asparagus stems; tomatoes; lettuce, such as romaine, endive, and radicchio; carrot and celery ends; bell or sweet pepper ends and seeds; mushroom stems; spinach; and zucchini. Avoid starchy vegetables such as potatoes or vegetables from the cabbage family—including all types of cabbage, kale, and even Brussels sprouts—as they can become bitter.

• For a classic spice combo, use ½ teaspoon each rosemary, thyme, basil, and oregano.

Easy Black Bean Soup

I started making an easy

black bean soup on the stove top: canned beans, salsa, and veggie broth. This is an equally simple version for the pressure cooker.

1 cup (200 g) dried black beans, soaked for 12 hours or overnight

1 teaspoon extra-virgin olive oil or 1/4 cup (60 ml) water or vegetable broth

1 carrot, diced

1 stalk celery, chopped

1/2 cup (80 g) diced onion

2 cloves garlic, minced

4 cups (940 ml) vegetable broth

1 cup (235 ml) water

1 cup (260 g) fresh salsa

Rinse the beans and drain well.

In an uncovered pressure cooker, heat the oil on medium-high. Add the carrot, celery, onion, and garlic and sauté for 1 minute. Add the beans, broth, water, and salsa. Stir to combine.

Cover and bring to pressure. Cook at high pressure for 4 to 6 minutes. Allow for a natural release.

Yield: 4 to 6 servings

Garam Masala Lentil Soup

Garam masala and cinnamon

fill this simple recipe with flavor.

1 3/4 cups (350 g) dried brown or green lentils

1 tablespoon (15 ml) vegetable oil

2 tablespoons (20 g) finely diced shallot

1 cup (130 g) diced carrots

1 cup (120 g) diced celery

1/2 teaspoon garam masala

1/2 teaspoon ground cinnamon

1/2 teaspoon cumin

1 bay leaf

2 cups (470 ml) vegetable broth

3 cups (705 ml) water

1/4 to 1/2 teaspoon sea salt (optional)

Freshly ground black pepper

Rinse and drain the lentils.

In an uncovered pressure cooker, heat the oil on medium heat. Add the shallot, carrots, and celery and sauté for 3 to 5 minutes, until the shallot and celery are soft. Add the garam masala, cinnamon, cumin, bay leaf, and lentils and stir well. Add the vegetable broth and water and stir to combine.

Cover and bring to pressure. Cook at high pressure for 7 to 10 minutes. Allow for a natural release.

Remove the cover and stir in the salt to taste. Remove the bay leaf before serving. Serve with freshly ground black pepper.

Yield: 6 servings

White Beans and Greens Soup

Packed with leafy greens and beans, this soup is a nutrient-dense meal. It's lightly seasoned so that you can play with flavors you love by stirring them in after tasting. During a recent cooking class my students opted for balsamic vinegar and ground black pepper to bring out the sweet and spicy in the soup, and it was terrific. For something zestier, add chili powder or chipotle powder while cooking and stir in hot sauce before serving. I serve this soup over cooked quinoa to make this a filling dinner entrée.

1½ cups (300 g) dried cannellini beans, soaked for 12 hours or overnight

1 tablespoon (15 ml) vegetable oil (optional)

4 large cloves garlic, minced

2 cups (320 g) diced carrots

1 cup (160 g) diced onion

1 cup (120 g) diced celery

2 cups (140 g) sliced cremini, shiitake, maitake, or baby bella mushrooms

1 bay leaf

2 tablespoons (3 g) dried herbes de Provence

½ teaspoon freshly ground black pepper, plus more for serving

1 teaspoon red pepper flakes

5 cups (1.2 L ml) vegetable broth

2 cups (470 ml) water

¼ cup (64 g) tomato paste

8 cups (400 g) loosely packed greens

Juice of 1 large lemon (about 3 tablespoons, or 45 ml)

1 to 1½ teaspoons salt (optional)

Rinse and the drain beans.

In an uncovered pressure cooker, heat the oil on medium-high. Add the garlic, carrots, onion, and celery and sauté for 3 minutes. Add the mushrooms and seasonings and sauté for another 3 to 5 minutes. Add the vegetable broth, water, and tomato paste. Mix well. Add the beans and greens. Stir to combine.

Cover and bring to pressure. Cook at high pressure for 6 to 8 minutes. Allow for a natural release.

Remove the lid, stir in the lemon juice and taste before adding salt. Remove the bay leaf before serving. Serve with freshly ground black pepper

Yield: 6 servings

Recipe Note

Baby spinach, kale, bok choy, arugula, collard greens, and Swiss chard are all excellent greens in this soup; try a combo of three or four.

Curried Mung Bean Stew

The mung bean is often used in Asian cuisine. This quick-cooking legume is super-nutritious—packed with protein, dietary fiber, potassium, iron, and magnesium—and is fantastic in Indian-style fare. Curry bullion cubes are great for this, or mix 2 cups (470 ml) water with 2 teaspoons curry powder.

1 teaspoon vegetable oil

2 cloves garlic, minced

1 cup (160 g) diced onion

1/2 cup (65 g) chopped carrot

1 cup (110 g) cubed sweet potatoes

1/2 cup (60 g) chopped celery

3 cups (150 g) loosely packed collard green strips

1 teaspoon ground ginger or 1 tablespoon (6 g) minced fresh

1/4 teaspoon turmeric

1/4 teaspoon paprika

2 cups (470 ml) curry broth

1 cup (235 ml) water

1 cup (200 g) dried mung beans

2 tablespoons (45 ml) lemon juice

1/2 teaspoon sea salt

In an uncovered pressure cooker, heat the oil on medium heat, add the garlic, onion, carrot, potatoes, and celery and sauté for 5 minutes. Add the collard greens, ginger, turmeric, paprika, curry broth, water, and mung beans. Stir to combine.

Cover and bring to pressure. Cook at high pressure for 6 to 8 minutes. Allow for a natural release.

Stir in the lemon juice and add salt to taste.

Yield: 4 servings

Potato Soup

One of my all-time cherished food memories is my dad making a very simple potato soup: boiled potatoes, onions, and celery cooked in whole milk and butter. I love making familiar foods vegan, and this may be one of my favorites. Healthier and cooked in less than half the time, it warms my heart and belly just the same as the original.

2 to 3 tablespoons (28 to 42 g) vegan butter

3 cloves garlic, minced

1 package (14 ounces, or 392 g) soft tofu

1 cup (235 ml) almond milk

2 tablespoons (30 ml) lemon juice

1/2 teaspoon salt

1 teaspoon dried dill

4 cups (440 g) diced potatoes

2 cups (140 g) sliced mushrooms

2 cups (320 g) sliced onion, cut into half-moons

1 cup (130 g) chopped carrot

1 cup (120 g) chopped celery

4 cups (940 ml) vegetable broth

Ground black pepper, to taste

In an uncovered pressure cooker, heat the butter on medium-high heat. Add the garlic and sauté for a minute.

In a blender or food processor, pulse the tofu, almond milk, lemon juice, salt, and dill until creamy.

Add the potatoes, mushrooms, onion, carrots, and celery to the pressure cooker, mixing well. Pour the tofu mixture into the pressure cooker. Stir in the vegetable broth. (Tip: As a way to get the remaining tofu cream out of the blender, first pour the vegetable broth into the blender and pulse quickly; then pour into the pot.)

Cover and bring to pressure. Cook at high pressure for 5 minutes. Use a quick release. Serve with freshly ground black pepper.

Yield: 8 servings

Recipe Notes

• No need to press or drain the tofu in this recipe. Though harder to find at standard grocery stores, boxed silken tofu—typically found in the Asian foods aisle—works very well in this soup.

• Yam, sweet, or russet potatoes are terrific in this recipe; try using a combination of all three.

Creamy Kale Miso Soup

I created this soup for my book *Vegan for Her* and it became my
go-to cooking demonstration recipe at vegetarian food festivals and grocery stores. Why? It's simple and it's packed with nutrients. Don't worry about details when it comes to chopping and dicing because the soup will get transferred to the blender and those blades will do all the work.

1 to 2 teaspoons vegetable oil

4 cloves garlic, cut in half

1 small sweet onion, quartered

2 medium carrots, cut into
  2- to 3-inch (5 to 7.5 cm)
  pieces

4 cups (940 ml) low-sodium
  vegetable broth

1 package (12 ounces, or 344 g)
  package silken (light
  firm) tofu

1 bunch kale (about 6 ounces
  [168 g] off the stem), plus a
  few leaves for garnish

¼ cup (63 g) yellow miso

Ground black pepper, to taste

In an uncovered pressure cooker, heat the oil on medium-high. Add the garlic, onion, and carrots and sauté for 5 minutes (add liquid if it begins to stick). The onion pieces will begin to brown; this is a semicaramelizing step that brings out so much flavor. Stir frequently.

Add the vegetable broth and tofu. Crumble the tofu into pieces with a spoon. Add the kale and stir to combine.

Cover and bring to pressure. Cook at high pressure for 4 minutes. Allow for a natural release; if after 10 minutes the pressure has still not come down fully, manually release. Remove the lid and stir in the miso.

Transfer to a blender (no more than 3 cups [705 ml] of hot soup at a time) and blend for 20 to 30 seconds, until the kale leaves are completely blended. Note: Hot soup expands in the blender, so pay heed to using only 3 cups (705 ml) of soup at a time and place a hand towel over the top of the blender for an added measure of safety.

Serve with black pepper and garnish with extra kale.

Yield: 6 servings

Recipe Note

Because we're using miso in this recipe, low-sodium broth is very important—even better, use some of your own, no-sodium homemade broth.

Chik'n Lentil Noodle Soup

This soup is a reader favorite on my blog, I suspect because it is
reminiscent of a childhood favorite for many of us—and because it's incredibly easy to prepare and
delicious! The "chicken" flavoring is simply seasoning. I use Butler Chik-Style seasoning, though
your favorite brand of dry seasoning will do just fine. This is rich in protein and packed with
healthy vegetables.

1 teaspoon extra-virgin olive oil

3 cloves garlic, finely diced

1 large onion, diced

2 cups (200 g) green beans
(fresh or frozen), snapped
into bite-size pieces

1 cup (130 g) chopped carrots

1 cup (120 g) chopped celery

2 teaspoons vegan chicken-
flavored seasoning

1 bay leaf

$\frac{1}{2}$ teaspoon dried sage

1 cup (200 g) dried brown
lentils, rinsed and drained

4 ounces (112 g) soba noodles

4 cups (940 ml) vegetable broth

1 to 1$\frac{1}{2}$ cups (235 to 355 ml)
water

In an uncovered pressure cooker, heat the oil on
medium-high. Add the garlic, onions, green beans,
carrots, and celery and sauté for about 3 minutes. Add
the chicken-flavored seasoning, bay leaf, and sage and
sauté for another 2 minutes. Add the lentils, noodles,
vegetable both, and water. Stir to combine.

Cover and to bring to pressure. Cook at high pressure
for 8 minutes. Use a quick release.

Sample both the lentils and the noodles. If they are
not cooked through, simmer on low in the uncovered
pressure cooker until done, adding more water if
necessary. Remove the bay leaf before serving.

Yield: 4 to 6 servings

Recipe Notes

• You can find vegan chicken-style seasoning or
bouillon cubes at most grocery stores.

• To deepen the flavor further, use vegan chicken
broth instead of vegetable broth.

Portobello Mushroom and Barley Soup

The first time I made this recipe I felt like a culinary rock star: a homemade soup made with whole vegetables, whole grains, and my homemade vegetable stock made completely from more whole vegetables. Quick to prepare and quick to the table, this substantial soup stands alone as a lunch or dinner entrée.

1 teaspoon vegetable oil

2 cloves garlic, minced

½ cup (80 g) diced onion

3 stalks celery, chopped

2 carrots, diced

2 large portobello mushrooms (6 ounces [168 g]), sliced lengthwise, then sliced again

1 tomato, diced

¾ cup (200 g) pearl barley, rinsed and drained

3 cups (705 ml) vegetable broth

4 cups (940 ml) water

2 sprigs fresh thyme or 1 teaspoon dried

½ to 1 teaspoon salt

Ground black pepper

In an uncovered pressure cooker, heat the oil on medium-high. Add garlic and onion and sauté for 2 to 3 minutes, until the onion is soft. Add the celery and carrot and sauté for another 3 to 5 minutes, until the celery is soft. Add the mushrooms, tomato, barley, broth, water, and thyme. Stir to combine.

Cover and bring to pressure. Cook at high pressure for 20 minutes. Allow for a natural release.

Remove the cover and stir in the salt. Serve with freshly ground black pepper.

Yield: 6 to 8 servings

Recipe Note

You may use ¼ cup (60 ml) vegetable broth as a substitute for oil.

Very Veggie Split Pea Soup

The "very" in this recipe refers to the fresh green juice. If you don't
have a juicer, consider picking up 32 ounces (1 L) of your favorite liquefied vegetables at the local
market or juice bar. Using a vegetable broth is equally pleasing—choose a deeper, savory broth
such as mushroom or beef-flavored vegan.

4 cups (940 ml) fresh green
juice or low-sodium
vegetable broth

1 teaspoon vegetable or
extra-virgin olive oil

½ cup (80 g) diced onion

3 cloves garlic, minced

1 teaspoon ground rosemary

1 teaspoon coriander

1 teaspoon saffron strands

1 bay leaf

2 cups (400 g) dried split peas,
rinsed and drained

2 cups (470 ml) water

Juice of 1 lemon

½ to 1 teaspoon sea salt
(optional)

Ground black pepper

If you choose to use juice, make your favorite green
juice. Mine is 2 golden beets, 5 kale leaves, 6 Swiss chard
leaves, 1 cucumber, 1 zucchini, and 6 stalks of celery. This
should make approximately 4 cups (940 ml) green juice;
if not, add water to make up 4 cups (940 ml).

In an uncovered pressure cooker heat the oil on
medium-high. Add the onion and garlic and sauté for
2 to 3 minutes, until the onion is soft. Add the rosemary,
coriander, and saffron strands and stir well, covering the
onion and garlic. Add the bay leaf, split peas, vegetable
juice, and water. Stir to combine.

Cover and bring to pressure. Cook at high pressure for
6 minutes. Allow for a natural release.

Remove the bay leaf and stir in the lemon juice. Taste
before adding salt. Serve with freshly ground pepper.

Yield: 6 servings

Recipe Note

When cooking with saffron, a little goes a long way
and that's great because it's expensive! You might
not, however, experience its full flavor until the next
day. This soup is great reheated for leftovers.

Potato, Apple, and Lentil Soup

Sometimes I make recipes simply based on what I have in the refrigerator and pantry and similar cooking times. This is one of those recipes. I love apple and potato together. The apple adds a lightness to the soup and balances a heavy starch vegetable. And lentils are great in anything.

1 teaspoon extra-virgin olive oil

1 cup (160 g) diced onion

1 cup (130 g) chopped carrots

½ teaspoon chipotle powder

¼ teaspoon cayenne pepper

½ teaspoon ground cinnamon

3 cups (330 g) cubed potatoes

2 cups (300 g) diced apples

½ cup (100 g) dried brown lentils

4 cups (940 ml) low-sodium vegetable broth

½ to 1 teaspoon sea salt

Ground black pepper

In an uncovered pressure cooker, heat the oil on medium-high. Add the onion and carrots and sauté until the onions are soft, 3 to 4 minutes. Add the seasonings, potatoes, apples, lentils, and broth. Stir to combine.

Cover and bring to pressure. Cook at high pressure for 10 minutes. Allow for a natural release.

Remove the lid, taste and add salt to taste. Serve with freshly ground pepper.

Yield: 4 to 6 servings

Tofu, Chickpea, Artichoke, and Potato Soup

In this recipe I use canned chickpeas because sometimes you want quick cooking even quicker. This soup is marvelous served over greens—such as sautéed collard greens—and garnished with capers.

1 large potato, diced

3 cloves garlic, minced

½ package (14 ounces, or 392 g) extra-firm tofu, pressed, drained, and diced

1 can (14 ounces, or 392 g) chickpeas, rinsed and drained

1 can (14 ounces, or 392 g) artichoke hearts, drained

1 tomato, diced

2 stalks celery, chopped

1 teaspoon paprika

1 teaspoon turmeric

5 cups (1.2 L) vegetable broth

¼ teaspoon ground black pepper

¼ cup (34 g) capers, for garnish

Place the potato, garlic, tofu, chickpeas, artichokes, tomato, celery, paprika, turmeric, and broth in the pressure cooker. Stir to combine.

Cover and bring to pressure. Cook at high pressure for 6 minutes. Use a quick release.

Serve with freshly ground pepper and capers (about 1 tablespoon [8.5 g] per bowl).

Yield: 4 servings

Recipe Note
Save the other half of the tofu for a breakfast scramble or an "eggless" salad.

Bean and Barley Stew

This dish is easily a one-pot meal because it is packed with everything you need in a single sitting, but I still call it a stew because the mushrooms and barley add a soupy thickness that demands a spoon. If you can't find baby bella mushrooms, try portobello or cremini. Black, flageolet, or pinto beans are also terrific in place of the navy beans.

1 teaspoon extra-virgin olive oil

¼ cup (40 g) sliced shallot

2 stalks celery, diced

1 teaspoon seeded and minced fresh jalapeño

½ cup (35 g) sliced baby bella mushrooms

1 tomato, diced

1 cup (100 g) chopped green beans

1 bay leaf

1 teaspoon herbes de Provence

1 teaspoon dried thyme

1 teaspoon ground black pepper

4 cups (940 ml) low-sodium vegetable broth

3 cups (705 ml) water

1 cup (200 g) dried navy beans

¾ cup (150 g) dried pearl barley, rinsed and drained

Juice of 1 lemon

¼ teaspoon ground cardamom

½ to 1 teaspoon sea salt

In an uncovered pressure cooker, heat the oil on medium-high. Add the shallot, celery, and jalapeño and sauté for 3 minutes, until the celery is soft. Add the mushrooms, tomato, green beans, bay leaf, spices, broth, water, beans, and barley. Stir to combine.

Cover and bring to pressure. Cook at high pressure for 20 to 22 minutes. Allow a natural release.

Remove the lid and stir in the lemon juice, cardamom, and salt. If the beans are not quite done, simmer, uncovered, until cooked through. Remove the bay leaf before serving.

Yield: 6 servings

Vegan "Turkey," Bean, and Kale Soup

As an avid reader of food magazines and blogs, I have seen numerous turkey, kale, and white bean soup recipes. Already a lover of kale and beans, I decided to try a vegan version by using TVP—textured vegetable (soy) protein—as a ground meat replacement. This is very popular in my "multivore" home of one vegan and one omnivore.

1 teaspoon extra-virgin olive oil

½ cup (80 g) diced onion

2 tablespoons (20 g) minced garlic

1 cup (130 g) chopped carrots

1 cup (120 g) chopped celery

1 teaspoon ground cumin

1 teaspoon chili powder

1½ teaspoons dried oregano

1 tablespoon (8 g) chicken-flavored seasoning

½ cup (50 g) TVP

1 cup (200 g) dried Great Northern beans

4 cups (268 g) tightly packed kale, cut or torn into bite-size pieces

6 cups (1.4 L) low-sodium vegetable broth

4 cups (940 ml) water

2 tablespoons (32 g) tomato paste

2 tablespoons (30 ml) lemon juice

1 teaspoon sea salt

½ teaspoon ground black pepper

In an uncovered pressure cooker, heat the oil on medium-high. Add the onion and garlic and sauté for just 1 minute. Add the carrots and celery and sauté for another 2 to 3 minutes. Stir in the spices and chicken-flavored seasoning. Add the TVP, beans, kale, broth, and water. Stir to combine.

Cover and bring to pressure. Cook at high pressure for 25 to 30 minutes. Allow for a natural release.

Remove the lid and stir in the tomato paste, lemon juice, salt, and pepper. If the beans are not quite cooked through, simmer on low, with the pressure cooker uncovered, until done.

Yield: 4 servings

Recipe Notes

- You may substitute water or broth for the oil.
- This soup is great served with something spicy such as Sriracha, Louisiana hot sauce, or diced jalapeño.
- Try Butler Foods, Frontier, or McKay's chicken-style seasoning.

Cream of Asparagus and Potato Soup

This is one of my favorite soups in the early spring. Here in Colorado, we have wide-ranging weather. The addition of a spring asparagus to a comforting potato soup just seems to give me a little hope that longer, sunnier, warmer days are ahead.

1 tablespoon (14 g) vegan butter

1 small onion, chopped

2 cloves garlic, peeled and chopped

1 pound (454 g) asparagus, ends removed and chopped

1 large potato, peeled and diced (about 1½ cups)

4 ounces (112 g) shelf-stable extra-firm tofu (no need to press or drain)

2 cups (470 ml) not-chicken vegan broth

½ teaspoon ground black pepper

2 tablespoons (30 ml) lime (or lemon) juice

½ teaspoon salt, to taste (optional)

More pepper, to taste (I added another ½ teaspoon while blending)

Heat the butter in an uncovered Instant Pot or multi-cooker on the sauté function (adjust to less heat). Add the onion and garlic, and sauté for 3 minutes. Add the asparagus, potato, tofu, broth, and pepper. Cover the pot, move the sealing valve to sealing, select manual, toggle the pressure button to low pressure, and set to 4 minutes. Use a quick release once done.

Transfer the soup to a blender or food processor. Add the lime juice. Use a towel over the blender or top of the food processor to avoid an expansion the heat of the soup might produce. Pulse to a puree for only 30 seconds or so (You want a thick soup; I didn't go beyond #3 on the Vitamix.) Taste before adding salt and additional pepper.

Yield: 4 to 6 servings

Instant Pot Miso Soup

Traditional miso soup isn't so complicated, but to get the flavor in
the broth your vegetables need to cook for some time. Not so when pressure cooking! Note that
I want you to whisk the miso paste in broth after the cooking process. We didn't do this in the
Creamy Kale Miso Soup (page 72) because the soybean paste was for flavor. In this recipe, we want
the probiotic benefits of fermented miso so we make sure to add it after the cooking process is over
to keep those cultures alive.

1 small onion, cut into half-moon slices

2 medium carrots, chopped

2 medium stalks celery, chopped

1/2 cup (65 g) fresh or frozen corn

1 teaspoon wakame flakes

1 cup (240 g) silken tofu (lite firm or firm), cubed

4 cups (940 ml) water

2 tablespoons (32 g) white or yellow miso paste

Soy sauce, to taste

Combine the onion, carrots, celery, corn, wakame flakes, tofu, and water in the Instant Pot or multicooker. Cover the pot, move the steam release handle to sealing, select manual, toggle the pressure cooker button to low pressure, and set for 6 minutes. Use a quick release once done.

Remove the lid and spoon about one cup (235 ml) of the broth into a bowl or measuring cup. Add the miso paste to the hot broth and whisk until dissolved. Pour the miso broth back into the pot. Stir and serve. Add soy sauce to taste.

Yield: 4 servings

Anasazi Bean and Potato Soup

This colorful bean makes a far from ordinary potato soup! You may substitute pinto or cranberry beans for the anasazi beans, and/or regular potatoes for the fingerlings (though I love their creamy texture).

1 teaspoon extra-virgin olive oil

³/₄ cup (120 g) diced onion

3 cloves garlic, minced

2 tablespoons (18 g) diced jalapeño

½ teaspoon ground cumin

1 tablespoon (3 g) dried oregano

1 tablespoon (7 g) chili powder

1 teaspoon red pepper flakes

1 cup (150 g) diced yellow bell pepper

1½ cups (165 g) diced fingerling potatoes

2 cups (360 g) chopped fresh or canned diced tomatoes

½ teaspoon sea salt

2 bay leaves

6 cups (1.4 L) low-sodium vegetable broth

12 ounces (336 g) dried anasazi beans

2 tablespoons (30 ml) fresh lemon juice

In an uncovered pressure cooker, heat the oil on medium-high. Add the onion, garlic, jalapeño, cumin, oregano, chili powder, and red pepper flakes and sauté for 2 or 3 minutes. Add the bell pepper, potatoes, tomatoes, salt, bay leaves, vegetable broth, and beans. Stir to combine.

Cover and bring to pressure. Cook at low pressure for 22 to 25 minutes. Allow for a natural release.

Remove the lid, stir in the lemon juice, and do a taste test. If needed, add more salt. If the beans are not cooked through, simmer, uncovered, until done. Remove the bay leaves before serving.

Yield: 4 servings

Recipe Note

If you soak the beans overnight this soup cooks up in 7 minutes!

Speedy Bean Chili

Sometimes even I don't have the time to cook dried beans. This is one of my favorite chili recipes that, when cooked in the pressure cooker with canned or precooked beans, is done in 10 minutes! This chili is terrific served with a dollop of vegan sour cream.

1 teaspoon extra-virgin olive oil

1 cup (160 g) diced onion

3 cloves garlic, minced

½ cup (65 g) diced carrot

½ cup (60 g) chopped celery

1 cup (150 g) diced green bell pepper

1 cup (150 g) diced red bell pepper

1 seeded and finely diced fresh jalapeño

½ teaspoon cayenne pepper

1 teaspoon red pepper flakes

1 teaspoon chili powder

½ teaspoon ground cumin

1 can (28 ounces, or 784 g) diced tomatoes

2 tablespoons (36 g) tomato paste

2 cups (470 ml) low-sodium vegetable broth

1 cup (235 ml) water

1 can (14.5 ounces, or 406 g) whole kernel corn, drained

1 ½ cups (375 g) red kidney beans (cooked or canned), rinsed and drained

½ to 1 teaspoon sea salt (optional)

In an uncovered pressure cooker, heat the oil on medium-high. Add the onion, garlic, carrot, and celery and sauté for 3 minutes. Add the bell peppers, jalapeño, cayenne, red pepper flakes, chili powder, cumin, diced tomatoes, tomato paste, broth, water, corn, and beans.

Cover and bring to pressure. Cook at low pressure for 6 minutes. Allow for a natural release.

Remove the lid, taste, and add salt, if desired.

Yield: 4 servings

Recipe Note

Want to make this with a dried legume? Replace the cooked/canned kidney beans with dried brown lentils and cook for 10 minutes.

Black Bean and Sweet Potato Stew

Black beans and sweet potatoes are visually appealing (we eat with our eyes first!) with their vibrant color, but they are also a dynamic nutrition duo: Black beans are rich in calcium, protein, potassium, and magnesium and sweet potatoes—a slow carb—is a lower glycemic index food that releases glucose gradually and is rich in beta-carotene. And they taste great together!

4 cups plus 2 tablespoons (970 ml) vegetable broth, divided

½ cup (80 g) chopped onion

4 cloves garlic, minced

2 carrots, chopped

1 large sweet potato, diced into equal, bite-size pieces

3 stalks celery, chopped

2 small tomatoes, diced

½ teaspoon ground cinnamon

1 teaspoon garam masala

1 cup (200 g) dried black beans, rinsed and drained

2 bay leaves

½ teaspoon sea salt (optional)

¼ teaspoon black pepper

In an uncovered pressure cooker, heat the 2 tablespoons (30 ml) vegetable broth on high. Add the onion and garlic and sauté for about 2 minutes, until the onion is soft. Add the carrots and sweet potato and sauté for another 3 minutes.

Add the celery, tomatoes, cinnamon, and garam masala and stir to coat all of the vegetables with the spices. Add the black beans, bay leaves, and remaining 4 cups (940 ml) vegetable broth. Stir to combine.

Cover and bring to pressure. Cook at high pressure for 22 to 24 minutes. Allow for a natural release.

Remove the lid, remove the bay leaves, stir in the salt and pepper, and serve.

Yield: 6 servings

Kale, Lentil, and Squash Chili

It can be a challenge to rethink traditional chili of ground beef, red beans, and tomatoes. Kale and lentils are two of my favorite foods, and they go perfectly with squash, which makes for a creamy texture.

1 teaspoon vegetable oil

1/2 cup (80 g) diced onion

2 cloves garlic, minced

1/4 cup (38 g) diced green bell pepper

3 cups (450 g) diced butternut squash (1/2-inch, or 1.3 cm cubes)

1 1/2 teaspoons cumin

1 teaspoon chili powder

1 tablespoon (15 ml) Sriracha or other hot sauce

1 cup (200 g) dried brown lentils, rinsed and drained

2 tomatoes, diced

2 to 3 cups (470 to 705 ml) low-sodium vegetable broth, or more as needed

4 cups (268 g) loosely packed kale, cut or torn into bite-size pieces

1 tablespoon (15 ml) lemon juice

Salt and black pepper, to taste

In an uncovered pressure cooker, heat the oil on medium-high. Add the onion, garlic, and bell pepper and sauté for 2 to 3 minutes, until the onion softens. Add the squash, cumin, chili powder, and Sriracha and sauté for 3 to 5 minutes. Stir in the lentils and tomatoes.

Add enough vegetable broth to cover everything, then add more to cover by 1 inch (2.5 cm). Add the kale and stir to combine.

Cover and to bring to pressure. Cook at pressure for 8 to 10 minutes. Allow for a natural release.

Remove the lid. Return the uncovered pressure cooker back to low heat to simmer. Stir in the lemon juice. Add salt and ground black pepper to taste.

Yield: 6 servings

Recipe Note

If you like your chili extra hot, consider adding jalapeño or habanero peppers.

Flageolet Bean and Millet Stew

Flageolet beans are popular in French cuisine and particularly good in soups and salads. The green color of the beans, combined with a red apple and orange-hued millet, make for a colorful, rich stew.

1½ cups (300 g) dried flageolet beans, soaked for 12 hours or overnight

1 teaspoon extra-virgin olive oil

¼ cup sliced (40 g) shallot

½ cup (55 g) diced parsnip

1 gala or Red Delicious apple, diced

1 golden beet, diced

½ cup (80 g) millet

1 can (14 ounces, or 392 g) diced tomatoes

1 bay leaf

1 teaspoon whole fennel seed, crumbled

1 teaspoon dried thyme

1 teaspoon dried sweet basil

2½ cups (588 ml) vegetable broth, or more as needed

2½ cups (588 ml) water, or more as needed

1 to 2 tablespoons (15 to 30 ml) lemon juice

½ teaspoon sea salt (optional)

¼ to ½ teaspoon black pepper

Rinse and drain the beans.

In an uncovered pressure cooker, heat the oil on medium-high. Add the shallot and sauté for just 1 minute, just to soften a bit. Add the parsnip, apple, and beet and sauté for 3 to 5 minutes. Add the beans, millet, diced tomatoes, bay leaf, fennel, thyme, and basil. Stir to combine.

Because you want a stewlike consistency, you want enough liquid to cook but not too much. Cover the vegetables and beans with a 50:50 mixture of broth and water. Once covered, add more so that there are 3 inches (7.5 cm) of liquid over the beans.

Cover and bring to pressure. Cook at high pressure 10 minutes. Allow for a natural release.

Remove the lid and stir in the lemon juice. Taste and determine how much salt is needed, if any. Remove the bay leaf before serving. Add ground pepper and serve.

Yield: 4 to 6 servings

Split Pea and Barley Stew

This version of pea soup sticks to your bones because it's still packed with protein but the vitamins and nutrients and fiber in the grain boost the I-feel-full factor. And it tastes as good as it is good for you.

½ cup (60 g) chopped celery

2 cups (260 g) chopped carrots

3 cups (330 g) diced russet or Yukon gold potatoes (about 3 large potatoes)

1 ½ cups (240 g) half-moon slices onions

3 large cloves garlic, minced

1 teaspoon avocado or extra-virgin olive oil (optional)

¾ cup (150 g) dried split peas, rinsed and drained

¼ cup (150 g) dried pearled barley

1 cup (70 g) sliced baby bella mushrooms

1 bay leaf

½ teaspoon dried fennel seed, crumbled with your fingers

¼ teaspoon dried anise seed, crumbled with your fingers

1 teaspoon ground ginger

¾ teaspoon dried dill weed

1 tablespoon (14 g) tomato powder (or 2 tablespoons [32 g] tomato paste)

4 cups (940 ml) water

1 teaspoon sea salt (more or less, to taste)

½ teaspoon ground black pepper

Combine the celery, carrots, potatoes, onions, and garlic in the Instant Pot or multicooker. Drizzle avocado oil (if using) over the vegetables and sauté for 5 minutes (select sauté and use the default normal heat).

Add the split peas, barley, mushrooms, bay leaf, fennel, anise, ginger, dill, tomato powder, and water. Stir to mix well. Cover the pot, move the steam release handle to sealing, select manual (high pressure), and set for 7 minutes. Once done, allow for a natural release.

Remove the lid, stir in salt and pepper, and serve.

Yield: 6 servings

Refried Bean and Tempeh Soup (or Stew)

This hearty soup can be as spicy as you like—just add more or less jalapeño, green chilies, and chile peppers. You are also in the driver's seat for the texture. As written, this recipe tends more toward soup when hot out of the pot. The next day? It's thicker. But you can make it thicker right away: Mash 1 cup (242 g) of the refried beans and use ¾ to 1 cup (178 to 235 ml) of water instead of 1½ cups. Either way, if you're looking for a bowl of soup that feels like an entire meal, with a kick of heat, you're going to love this one.

1 teaspoon olive oil (or 2 to 3 teaspoons vegetable broth)

1 small onion, cut into half-moon slices

2 large cloves garlic, minced

1 ½ cups (355 ml) vegetable broth, divided

1 package (8 ounces, or 224 g) tempeh, quartered

1 can (15 ounces, or 425 g) pinto beans (or 1 ½ cups cooked pinto beans), rinsed and drained, divided

1 small jalapeño, seeded and finely diced

4 to 5 ounces (112 to 140 g) canned chopped or diced green chiles

1 can (14 ounces, or 392 g) fire-roasted diced tomatoes

1 ½ (355 ml) cups water

½ to 1 teaspoon chili powder (optional)

½ teaspoon chipotle or Ancho chile pepper

½ teaspoon salt

Heat the olive oil in an uncovered Instant Pot or multi-cooker on the sauté function (normal setting). Add the onion and garlic, and sauté for about 3 minutes. Add the quartered tempeh and ½ cup (120 ml) of the broth to the pot. Sauté and begin to crumble the tempeh with a wooden spoon. Prop the lid over the pot for 5 minutes. (Add vegetable broth as necessary to keep the tempeh from sticking.)

Meanwhile, in a small bowl, add ½ cup (121 g) of the pinto beans and all of the diced jalapeño. Mash with a potato masher or fork.

Continue to stir and sauté and crumble the tempeh until it resembles small white beans (or meatless crumbles). Transfer the mashed beans to the pot and, using the potato masher, mash into the tempeh.

Add the remaining whole beans, green chilies, tomatoes, water, chili powder (if using), and any remaining vegetable broth to the pot, combining well.

Cover the pot, move the steam release handle to sealing, select the manual function, toggle the pressure cooker button to low pressure, and set for 5 minutes. Once done, allow for a natural release.

Yield: 4 to 6 servings

Chunky Red Lentil Stew

This very quick, thick stew is fantastic served over grains such as barley, faro, or freekeh and is incredibly nutritious. Lentils are a good source of fiber, protein, iron, calcium, zinc, and B vitamins and cooked tomatoes offer lycopene, a health-promoting antioxidant.

2 cups plus 2 tablespoons (500 ml) vegetable broth, divided

2 cloves garlic, minced

1/2 cup (80 g) diced yellow onion

2 carrots, chopped

1/2 teaspoon garam masala

1/2 teaspoon curry powder

1 tomato, cut into large chunks

1 cup (200 g) dried red lentils, rinsed and drained

Juice of 1/2 lemon

Sea salt, to taste

In an uncovered pressure cooker, heat the 2 tablespoons (30 ml) vegetable broth on high. Add the garlic and onion and sauté for 2 to 3 minutes, until the onion is soft. Stir in the carrots, garam masala, and curry powder and sauté for another 2 to 3 minutes. Add the tomato, lentils, and remaining 2 cups (470 ml) vegetable broth. Stir to combine.

Cover and bring to pressure. Cook at high pressure for 6 minutes. Use a quick release.

Remove the lid and stir in the lemon juice, taste, and add salt, as needed.

Yield: 4 servings

Black-Eyed Pea and Collard Green Chili

The combination of this legume and leafy green sounds like a typical Southern dish and understandably, because in the South it is considered good luck to consume together on New Year's Day. A colorful dish, the protein-rich black-eyed pea and calcium-rich collard greens are also high in iron.

4 large collard green leaves

1 teaspoon extra-virgin olive oil

1/2 cup (80 g) diced red onion

3 cloves garlic, minced

2 cups (260 g) chopped carrot

2 cups (240 g) chopped celery

2 tablespoons (12 g) chili powder

1 teaspoon ground cumin

1/2 teaspoon ground coriander

1 teaspoon ground cinnamon

1 tablespoon (3 g) dried oregano

1 teaspoon seeded and diced fresh jalapeño

2 cups (400 g) dried black-eyed peas, rinsed and drained

2 bay leaves

1 can (28 ounces, or 784 g) diced tomatoes

1 can (8 ounces, or 224 g) tomato sauce

2 cups (470 ml) vegetable broth

1 cup (235 ml) water

1/4 to 1/2 teaspoon sea salt (optional)

Halve each collard leaf lengthwise with kitchen shears or a sharp knife, cutting out and discarding the center ribs. Stack the leaves and cut crosswise into 1/4-inch (6 mm) wide strips.

In an uncovered pressure cooker heat the oil on medium-high. Add the onion and garlic and sauté for about 2 minutes, until the onion begins to soften. Add the carrots and celery and continue to sauté for another 3 to 5 minutes. Add the collard greens, chili powder, cumin, coriander, cinnamon, oregano, and jalapeño and sauté for a minute or two. Add the black-eyed peas, bay leaves, diced tomatoes, tomato sauce, broth, and water. Stir to combine.

Cover and bring to pressure. Cook at high pressure for 10 minutes. Allow for a natural release.

Remove the cover and taste the black-eyed peas. Add salt to taste. If they are not thoroughly cooked, simmer on low, uncovered, until done. Remove the bay leaves before serving.

Yield: 4 to 6 servings

Asian Adzuki Bean Chili

The first time I used adzuki beans I researched them and learned that they are popular in Japanese cuisine. This inspired me to think about other Eastern-influenced flavors and seasoning to make a different kind of chili.

1½ cups (300 g) dried adzuki beans, soaked for 12 hours or overnight

1 tablespoon (15 ml) sesame oil

3 or 4 large cloves garlic, minced

1 cup (160 g) diced onion

1 cup (130 g) chopped carrots

4 cups (940 ml) vegetable broth

1 can (14 ounces, or 392 g) fire-roasted diced tomatoes

2 tablespoons (32 g) tomato paste

1 teaspoon Herbamare

1 teaspoon dulse flakes

1 tablespoon (15 ml) yuzu pepper sauce

1 tablespoon (15 ml) low-sodium soy sauce

2 cups (180 g) sliced cabbage

Rinse and drain the beans.

In an uncovered pressure cooker, heat the oil on medium heat. Add the garlic, onion, and carrots and sauté for 3 minutes, until the onion is soft. Add the broth, beans, tomatoes, tomato paste, Herbamare, dulse, pepper sauce, soy sauce, and cabbage. Stir to combine.

Cover and bring to pressure. Cook at high pressure for 7 minutes. Allow for a natural release.

Yield: 6 servings

Recipe Notes

• Herbamare and dulse flakes (a sea vegetable) are salt alternatives with an Asian flare. Dulse flakes can be found in the Asian section of the grocery store; if you can't find them, try wakame, arame, or hijiki (other types of sea vegetables).

• Yuzu pepper sauce is a Japanese hot sauce; you can substitute your favorite hot sauce.

Summer Lentil and Millet Chili

This chili pulls together what I consider to be the three vegan meal essentials: beans, greens, and grains. Summer vegetables fresh from the garden and light lentils with quick-to-cook millet make this chili perfect in the summer, no matter how hot the day.

2 tablespoons (30 ml) olive oil

1 cup (160 g) finely diced yellow onion

2 cloves garlic, minced

1 seeded and finely diced fresh jalapeño

½ teaspoon ground cinnamon

1 teaspoon chili powder

1 teaspoon ground cumin

1 bay leaf

½ cup (60 g) diced summer squash (lightly peeled, if needed)

4 cups (720 g) diced fresh tomatoes

2 cups (134 g) tightly packed bite-size pieces kale

1 cup (200 g) dried brown lentils, rinsed and drained

1 cup (88 g) millet, rinsed and drained

2 cups (470 ml) low-sodium vegetable broth

4 cups (940 ml) water

Juice of 1 lemon

1 tablespoon (2 g) chopped fresh sweet basil, plus more for garnish

½ teaspoon sea salt, or to taste

Heat the olive oil in a 6-quart (6 L) or larger pressure cooker (if your pressure cooker is smaller, reduce the quantity of chili by half). Add the onion and cook for 3 to 4 minutes, stirring occasionally, until softened. Add the garlic, stir, then add the jalapeño, cinnamon, chili powder, and cumin and sauté for a few minutes more, until the jalapeño softens. Add the bay leaf, squash, tomatoes, kale, lentils, millet, broth, and water and stir to combine.

Cover and bring to high pressure (this will take a while because the pressure cooker is loaded with veggies, lentils, grains, and liquid). Once high pressure is achieved, lower the heat to maintain pressure. Cook at pressure for 8 minutes. Remove from the burner and allow for a natural release.

Once the pressure is released, carefully remove the lid, pointing it away from you. Place back on the burner, uncovered, on low heat and bring to a simmer, then add the lemon juice, basil, and salt.

Stir and let simmer for a few minutes more. Garnish with additional fresh basil.

Yield: 6 to 8 servings

CHAPTER FOUR

One-Pot Meals

Raise your hand if you bought your pressure cooker because you wanted to make one-pot meals? My hand is raised! Although I love using my rice and slow cookers, I am constantly seduced by the speed of a pressure cooker. These meals are done in minutes, yet taste like they've been cooking for hours!

Black Beans and Quinoa, page 104

Navy Beans, Rice, and Greens, page 105

New World Székely Goulash, page 106

Quinoa-Millet-Pea Bowl, page 108

Amaranth Lentils, page 110

Black Beans and Yams, page 111

Gingered Adzuki Beas, Greens, and Grains, page 111

Quick-and-Easy Rice and Peas, page 112

Breakfast (or not) Bean & Potato Hash, page 113

Vegan "Bacon" and Cabbage, page 114

Korean Kongbap, page 116

Lentil, Kale, and Barley Risotto, page 118

Fava Bean Risotto, page 120

Black-Eyed Peas and Farro, page 121

Soy Curl Mac 'n Cheese, page 122

Taco Mac 'n Cheese, page 124

Sweet Red Lentil Coconut Curry, page 126

Seitan Swiss Steak, page 128

Tofu Scramble, page 130

Black Beans and Quinoa

This one-pot meal is great as an entrée served over raw or sautéed greens, and it also makes a great side dish with grilled or baked tofu or tempeh. Try it cold as a filling wrapped in raw collard greens or in a tortilla wrap sandwich.

1 cup (200 g) dried black beans, soaked for 12 hours or overnight

1 cup (130 g) diced carrot

¼ cup (40 g) diced sweet onion

1 clove garlic, minced

1 ½ cups (265 g) quinoa

1 teaspoon chili powder

2 cups (470 ml) low-sodium vegetable broth

½ teaspoon sea salt (optional)

Add all the ingredients to the pressure cooker. Stir to combine. Cover and bring to pressure. Cook at high pressure for 6 minutes. Allow for a natural release.

Yield: 4 servings

Navy Beans, Rice, and Greens

Another simple beans, greens, and grains recipe—this time with
quick-cooking rice and calcium-rich kale—that is filling and cooks up in no time. Serve as an entrée
and use the leftovers as a side dish for another meal.

1 cup (200 g) dried navy
beans, soaked for 12 hours
or overnight

1 teaspoon vegetable oil

½ cup (80 g) diced red onion

3 cloves garlic, minced

½ cup (95 g) short-grain
white rice

4 cups (280 g) loosely
packed bite-size pieces
kale

1 bay leaf

1 teaspoon dried thyme

2 ½ cups (588 ml) water,
or more as needed

1 tablespoon (15 ml)
lemon juice

½ to 1 teaspoon sea salt

Rinse and drain the beans.

In an uncovered pressure cooker, heat the oil on
medium-high. Add the onion and garlic and sauté for 3
minutes, until the onion is soft. Add the beans, rice, kale,
bay leaf, thyme, and water to cover.

Cover and bring to pressure. Cook at high pressure for
6 to 8 minutes. Allow for a natural release.

Remove the lid, remove and discard the bay leaf, and
stir in the lemon juice and salt.

Yield: 4 servings

Recipe Notes

- If you don't have time to soak the navy beans,
  proceed with the dried beans, increase the water
  by ½ cup (120 ml), and cook for 22 minutes total.

- For a leafy green alternative, substitute baby
  spinach or shredded collard greens for the kale.

New World Székely Goulash

Early in our marriage, my half-Hungarian husband introduced me to "old world" goulash made with sauerkraut, pork, and sour cream. This was foreign to me, the girl who was raised in rural Illinois and knew goulash as elbow macaroni, ground beef, and tomatoes. This recipe is a blend of the traditional Székely goulash ingredients—specifically the sauerkraut and sour cream—with the Midwest addition of tomatoes. The chickpeas stand in as the protein replacement for the pork.

1 cup (200 g) dried chickpeas, soaked for 12 hours or overnight

1 teaspoon extra-virgin olive oil

2 cloves garlic, minced

1/2 cup (80 g) half-moon slices yellow onion

1 1/2 cups (195 g) chopped carrots

2 tablespoons (14 g) paprika, plus more for garnish

1 teaspoon freshly ground black pepper, plus more for serving

2 cups (470 ml) vegetable broth

1 cup (245 g) tomato sauce

1 bay leaf

1 to 1 1/2 cups (235 to 355 ml) water, or as needed

1 teaspoon sea salt

32 ounces (896 g) sauerkraut, drained

1/2 cup (120 g) vegan sour cream

Rinse and drain the chickpeas.

In an uncovered pressure cooker, heat the olive oil on medium-high heat. Add the garlic, onion, and carrots and sauté for 3 minutes, until the onion softens. Stir in the paprika and black pepper. Add the chickpeas, vegetable broth, tomato sauce, bay leaf, and enough water to cover everything, plus an additional 1/2 inch (1.3 cm).

Cover and bring to pressure. Cook at high pressure for 13 to 15 minutes. Allow for a natural release.

Remove the cover and stir in the salt. If the chickpeas are not quite done, simmer on low until thoroughly cooked. Remove and discard the bay leaf.

Stir in the sauerkraut and vegan sour cream and simmer on low until everything is completely heated through. Garnish with a dash of paprika and serve with freshly ground black pepper.

Yield: 6 servings

Quinoa-Millet-Pea Bowl

This recipe is lightly seasoned to allow the contrasting textures of the peas, grains, and vegetables to come through. Rosemary offers a hint of seasoning to this light yet substantial meal.

½ cup (100 g) dried whole peas, soaked for 12 hours or overnight

½ cup (60 g) sliced zucchini

½ cup (60 g) chopped celery

¼ cup (40 g) finely diced onion

1 cup (175 g) quinoa, rinsed and drained

½ cup (90 g) millet, rinsed and drained

2 cups (470 ml) vegetable broth

½ to 1 cup (120 to 235 ml) water

1 teaspoon whole rosemary, crumbled

½ to 1 teaspoon sea salt

Rinse and drain the peas. Place all the ingredients, except the salt, in the pressure cooker. Stir to combine.

Cover and bring to pressure. Cook at high pressure for 8 to 10 minutes. Allow for a natural release.

Remove the lid and stir in the salt to taste. Fluff up the millet with a fork. Leave uncovered for about 5 minutes, then fluff again before serving.

Yield: 4 to 6 servings

Recipe Note

Adzuki, Great Northern, or kidney beans are good substitutes for peas if you want to add more protein to this dish.

Amaranth Lentils

I consider this a power dish—or is it a power bowl? It's packed with protein, fiber, iron, calcium, magnesium, and more! Nutrient-dense, the texture is nice and light.

1 teaspoon vegan butter

2 cloves garlic, minced

¼ cup (40 g) diced yellow onion

½ cup (100 g) amaranth

½ cup (100 g) dried
   brown lentils

2 cups (140 g) shredded
   Swiss chard

2 to 2¼ cups (470 to 530 ml)
   water, or as needed

¼ teaspoon ground coriander

½ teaspoon sea salt

¼ cup (25 g) chopped scallion

In an uncovered pressure cooker, melt the butter on medium heat. Add the garlic and onion and sauté until the onion is soft, about 3 minutes. Add the amaranth, lentils, and Swiss chard and stir to combine. Add the water: Start with 2 cups (470 ml) water and add enough to cover everything. Stir to combine.

Cover and bring to pressure. Cook at high pressure for 8 to 10 minutes. Allow for a natural release.

Remove the cover and stir in the coriander and salt. Garnish with the scallion.

Yield: 4 servings

Recipe Note

Collard greens, turnip greens, and kale are all great substitutes for Swiss chard.

Black Beans and Yams

Why use canned beans in the pressure cooker? Because sometimes you forget to soak your beans and you *still* want dinner in less than 10 minutes! Serve these black beans and yams over a bed of arugula or sautéed kale to get your leafy greens!

2 cups (220 g) diced yams

1 cup (235 ml) vegetable broth

1/2 cup (130 g) salsa (jarred, fresh, or homemade)

1 can (14 ounces, or 392 g) black beans, rinsed and drained

Add all the ingredients to the pressure cooker. Cover and bring to pressure. Cook at high pressure for 4 minutes. Use a quick release.

Yield: 2 to 4 servings

Gingered Adzuki Beans, Greens, and Grains

Inspired by Lorna Sass's *Gingered Adzuki Squash Stew* recipe, this is a one-pot hippie bowl meal!

1 teaspoon sesame oil

2 or 3 cloves garlic, minced

1 teaspoon grated ginger

1/2 cup (35 g) sliced maitake or shiitake mushrooms

2 cups (140 g) shredded collard greens, Swiss chard, kale, or a mix

1 cup (200 g) dried adzuki beans

1/2 cup (95 g) brown rice

1-inch (2.5 cm) strip kombu

3 cups (705 ml) water

3 umeboshi plums, mashed with a fork

1 tablespoon (15 ml) lemon juice

1 tablespoon (15 ml) tamari

In an uncovered pressure cooker, heat the oil on medium-high. Add the garlic and ginger and sauté for 2 minutes, until the garlic is softened. Stir in the mushrooms, greens, adzuki beans, brown rice, kombu, and water.

Cover and bring to pressure. Cook at high pressure for 22 minutes. Allow for a natural release.

Remove the cover and stir. Return to the burner, turn the heat to low, and simmer while stirring in the mashed umeboshi plums, lemon juice, and tamari (about 3 minutes).

Yield: 4 to 6 servings

Quick-and-Easy Rice and Peas

True story: I created this recipe on a Saturday night. It was 5:30 p.m. and I had no idea what to make for dinner. One quick scan of the pantry and I grabbed a bag of white rice and a bag of black-eyed peas and at 6 p.m. we were eating dinner.

1 teaspoon extra-virgin olive oil

1 large onion, diced

2 large carrots, diced

3 medium celery stalks, diced

3 large cloves garlic, minced

1 medium tomato, diced

1 cup (200 g) dried black-eyed peas

½ cup (95 g) long-grain white rice

1 teaspoon dried parsley

1 teaspoon dried oregano

1 teaspoon dried crushed red pepper

¼ teaspoon ground black pepper

¼ teaspoon ground cumin

¼ cup (64 g) tomato paste

2 to 2½ cups (470 to 588 ml) low-sodium vegetable broth

Juice from 1 small lemon (about 2 tablespoons)

Sea salt, to taste

Heat the oil in an uncovered Instant Pot or multicooker on the sauté function (normal). Add the onion, carrots, celery, and garlic, and sauté for 5 minutes. Add the tomato, black-eyed peas, rice, parsley, oregano, red pepper, black pepper, cumin, and tomato paste. Combine well. Begin adding the broth until there's enough liquid to cover everything, plus a little more. Stir to combine well. Cover, move the steam release handle to sealing, select manual (high pressure), and set to 8 minutes. Once done, allow for a natural release.

Remove the cover and stir in the fresh lemon juice. If the black-eyed peas or rice are not quite done, simmer on the sauté function (normal) until cooked.

Add salt, if desired.

Yield: 4 servings

Breakfast (or not)
Bean & Potato Hash

Many vegans who love their Instant Pots also really love Rancho

Gordo beans—it's rather cultlike, actually. I'm a fan of the heirloom beans, too, but I offer a couple of other dried bean options in the note. This one-pot meal is great for breakfast, lunch, or dinner. Just be sure to soak your beans the night before.

1 tablespoon avocado or extra-virgin olive oil

4 cloves garlic, minced

3 cups (330 g) diced potatoes

2 cups (300 g) diced red and yellow pepper

1 cup (120 g) diced celery

1 cup (185 g) Rancho Gordo Scarlet Runner beans, soaked overnight (rinsed and drained)

2 to 2 1/2 cups (470 to 588 ml) vegetable broth (or water)

1 tablespoon (4 g) dried Mexican oregano (or other oregano)

1 teaspoon chili powder

Salt, to taste

Fresh oregano, for garnish

Heat oil in an uncovered Instant Pot or multicooker on the sauté function (normal). Add the garlic, potatoes, peppers, and celery, and sauté for 3 to 5 minutes. Add the beans. Begin adding broth or water until there's just enough liquid to cover the beans. Stir in the dried oregano and chili powder. Cover the pot, set valve to sealing, select manual (high pressure), and set the time to 11 or 12 minutes. Once done, allow for a natural release.

Remove the cover and test the beans for doneness. If not quite cooked through, simmer uncovered on the sauté function (normal) until the beans are done and/or the liquid is absorbed. Salt, to taste.

Yield: 4 servings

Recipe Note

To substitute the Ayocote Morado beans, use soaked cannellini beans and cook for 6 to 8 minutes, or use soaked great Northern beans and cook for 7 to 10 minutes.

Vegan "Bacon" and Cabbage

I had a vegetarian "oops" moment years ago in Ireland. I ordered the cabbage and, unbeknownst to me, bacon is a standard ingredient in their version. Since then, I've created a simple, plant-based version that cooks up quickly and is sure to wow your omnivore friends and family.

4 tablespoons (55 g) vegan butter

1 package (5 ounces, or 140 g) vegan bacon, cut into ½-inch (1.3 cm) pieces

1 sweet onion, cut into half-moon slices

2 potatoes, peeled and diced into bite-size cubes

1 head cabbage, cored and thinly sliced (about 1½ pounds, or 680 g)

1 tablespoon (7 g) smoked paprika

1½ cups (355 ml) vegan chicken-flavored broth

Salt and freshly ground black pepper, to taste

In an uncovered pressure cooker, melt the butter on medium-high. Add the bacon pieces and stir well to cover with the butter. Add the onion and sauté until soft, about 3 minutes. Add the potatoes, cabbage, and paprika. Add the broth and stir to combine.

Cover and bring to pressure. Cook at high pressure for 4 minutes. Allow for a natural release.

Remove the cover and add salt and pepper to taste.

Yield: 6 servings

Recipe Notes

• Because vegan bacon will not have "drippings," vegan butter adds liquid to the sauté process. You can substitute 1 to 2 tablespoons (15 to 30 ml) extra-virgin olive oil or ¼ to ½ cup (60 to 120 ml) vegetable broth.

• You can find vegan chicken-flavored broth at many grocery stores, or heat 1½ cups (355 ml) water with vegan chicken-flavored bouillon.

Korean Kongbap

Kongbap is a Korean dish comprising white or brown rice cooked with one or more beans (and sometimes also other grains). This basic recipe is true to the traditional dish—beans and grains with no spices, though I do use sesame oil for both flavor and to avoid possible foaming. Serve this over a bed of sautéed greens with soy sauce and a garnish of freshly grated ginger, as a side dish with a generous helping of your favorite hot sauce, such as Sriracha, or as an appetizer rolled up in a nori sheet for a Korean kongbap sushi roll—just dip in soy sauce with wasabi.

½ cup (100 g) dried
   black soybeans

½ cup (100 g) dried whole peas

½ cup (95 g) brown rice

½ cup (100 g) pearl barley

7 to 7½ cups (1.6 to 1.8 L) water,
   divided

1 tablespoon (15 ml) sesame oil

Combine the soybeans, peas, brown rice, and pearl barley to a large bowl and add 4 cups (940 ml) of the water. Soak overnight.

Rinse, drain, and add to the pressure cooker. Add the remaining 3 to 3½ cups (705 to 825 ml) water. Drizzle the oil over the water. Stir to combine.

Cover and bring to pressure. Cook at high pressure for 22 minutes. Allow for a natural release; if after 10 minutes the pressure has still not come down fully, manually release.

Yield: 6 servings

Recipe Note

This is the consummate bulk-cooked recipe—you can add it to soups, salads, stir-fries, and more.

Lentil, Kale, and Barley Risotto

This longer cooking risotto features pearl barley. The first time I made this dish I was deep into half-marathon training and this was my go-to "carbo-load" meal. Serve this as an entrée or as a side dish with baked tofu. Please note that this calls for cooked lentils, which you can make in advance.

4 teaspoons (20 ml) extra-virgin olive oil

¼ cup (40 g) diced onion

2 cloves garlic, minced

1 teaspoon seeded and diced fresh jalapeño

1 cup (200 g) dried pearl barley

2 cups (470 ml) vegetable broth, or more as needed

1 cup (235 ml) water, or more as needed

¼ teaspoon sea salt, plus more to taste

¼ teaspoon black pepper, plus more to taste

2 cups (340 g) cooked lentils

2 cups (140 g) tightly packed chopped kale

2 to 3 tablespoons (30 to 45 ml) lemon juice

¼ cup (24 g) nutritional yeast

2 teaspoons grated vegan Parmesan cheese

1 teaspoon dried sweet basil

In an uncovered pressure cooker, heat the oil on medium-high. Add the onion, garlic, and jalapeño and sauté for 3 minutes, until the onion is soft. Add the barley, vegetable broth, water, salt, and pepper. Stir to combine.

Cover and bring to pressure. Cook at high pressure for 18 to 20 minutes. Use a quick release.

Remove the lid and stir in the cooked lentils, kale, lemon juice, nutritional yeast, Parmesan cheese, and basil. Simmer on low for approximately 10 minutes or to the desired risotto consistency (add more vegetable broth or water if needed). Taste and season with salt and pepper.

Yield: 6 to 8 servings

Fava Bean Risotto

I include two risotto recipes in this book, and both contain legumes. This recipe is excellent with or without a legume, but as a one-pot meal, the addition of fresh fava beans provides an inexpensive lean protein element to the dish.

1 tablespoon (14 g) vegan butter

3 cloves garlic, minced

¼ cup (40 g) diced onion

¼ cup (18 g) diced mushrooms

1 cup (125 g) fresh fava beans

1 cup (125 g) Arborio rice

2 cups (470 ml) vegetable broth

1¼ cups (295 ml) water

2 tablespoons (10 g) grated vegan Parmesan cheese

2 tablespoons (14 g) nutritional yeast

½ to 1 teaspoon sea salt

In an uncovered pressure cooker melt the butter on medium-high. Add the garlic and onion and sauté for 3 minutes, until the onion is soft. Add the mushrooms, fava beans, and rice and stir to cover with the butter. Add the vegetable broth and water. Stir to combine.

Cover and bring to pressure. Cook at high pressure for 7 minutes. Use a quick release.

Remove the cover and stir in the Parmesan cheese, nutritional yeast, and salt to taste.

Yield: 4 servings

Black-Eyed Peas and Farro

Black-eyed peas and collard greens, when eaten on New Year's Day, are said to bring great fortune. True or not, they are a culinary match made in heaven. The first time I made this dish I rolled it up in large, raw collard green leaves (a crunchy, healthy alternative to a tortilla wrap), but it's also great over sautéed collard green strips.

2 tablespoons (30 ml) extra-virgin olive oil

1/2 cup (80 g) diced yellow onion

3 cloves garlic, chopped

2/3 cup (132 g) farro, rinsed

1/2 teaspoon crumbled dried thyme leaves

1/2 teaspoon dried sweet basil

3/4 cup (150 g) dried black-eyed peas

1 cup (235 ml) low-sodium vegetable broth

1 cup (235 ml) water

1 tablespoon (15 ml) soy sauce, tamari, or Bragg Liquid Aminos

1/2 teaspoon Sriracha or other hot sauce

In an uncovered pressure cooker, heat the oil on medium-high. Add the onion and garlic and sauté for 3 minutes, until the onion is translucent. Stir in the farro, thyme, and basil, then add the black-eyed peas, broth, and water. Stir to combine.

Cover and bring to pressure, then reduce the heat to maintain pressure. Cook at pressure for 10 minutes. Allow for a natural release.

Remove the lid and stir in the soy sauce and Sriracha.

Yield: 4 servings

Soy Curl Mac 'n Cheese

Soy curls, a textured vegetable protein food, are used in place of chicken in dishes such as stir-fries, casseroles, tacos, salads, and more. In this quick and easy vegan version of macaroni and cheese, the legume meat substitute adds protein, flavor, and density to a memorable comfort food.

This dish is fantastic with just the nutritional yeast, but if you're looking for something "cheesier," perhaps to impress non-vegan friends or family, stir in your favorite vegan cheese.

2 cups (200 g) soy curls

2 cups (470 ml) warm water plus 2 cups (470 ml) cold water, or more as needed, divided

2 tablespoons (28 g) vegan butter

1 cup (160 g) diced onion

2 cloves garlic, minced

2 tablespoons (16 g) vegan chicken-flavored seasoning

¼ to ½ teaspoon black pepper

1 cup (105 g) spelt elbow pasta

2 tablespoons (14 g) nutritional yeast

½ to 1 teaspoon salt

2 ounces (56 g) shredded vegan cheese (optional)

Rehydrate the soy curls by placing them in a large bowl and cover with the 2 cups (470 ml) warm water. Let sit for 10 minutes. Drain the excess liquid and set aside.

In an uncovered pressure cooker, heat the butter on medium-high. Add the onion and garlic and sauté for 3 minutes, until the onion is translucent. Stir in the soy curls, chicken-flavored seasoning, and pepper. Sauté for about 5 minutes. If the soy curls begin to stick to the pressure cooker, add 1 tablespoon (15 ml) water or vegetable broth.

Add the pasta and remaining 2 cups (470 ml) cold water, or as needed to cover the pasta. Stir in the nutritional yeast, and pat the soy curls and pasta down under the water.

Cover and bring to pressure. Cook at low pressure for 5 minutes. Use a quick release.

Remove the lid and taste before adding salt. Add the cheese and mix well. Let stand for 5 minutes to allow it to set up for a firmer consistency before serving.

Yield: 2 servings

Recipe Note

You can try other whole-grain pasta varieties; just make sure the cooking times listed on the package are similar to that of the spelt.

Taco Mac 'n Cheese

My vegan husband sometimes misses meat, but not enough to eat it. So we occasionally work vegan meats into our meals—soy curls being the number one choice. Now the maker of those curls, Butler Foods, has taco crumbles made from whole, non-GMO, organic soy beans. If you can't find them, no worries. Use your favorite spicy meatless crumbles from the frozen foods section (and omit the ½ cup [120 ml] water), or use TVP and add your favorite spices for tacos!.

½ cup (50 g) vegan taco crumbles (or TVP with added taco seasoning)

½ cup (120 ml) warm water

1 teaspoon organic canola oil

1 teaspoon minced garlic

1 small onion, diced

1 small green pepper, diced

1½ cups (157 g) quinoa elbow macaroni

1 can (14 ounces, or 392 g) fire-roasted tomatoes with chipotle peppers

1½ cups (355 ml) vegetable broth

¼ cup (24 g) nutritional yeast

¼ cup (28 g) crumbled vegan mozzarella

Fresh cilantro, for garnish (optional)

Rehydrate the taco crumbles: Place the crumbles (or TVP) in a medium bowl and pour the warm water over them. Stir to be sure all crumbles are in the water.

Heat the oil in an uncovered Instant Pot or multi-cooker on the sauté function (normal heat). Add the garlic and onion, and sauté for 2 or 3 minutes. Add the green pepper and sauté for a few minutes longer. Add the rehydrated taco crumbles, macaroni, tomatoes, and vegetable broth. Cover, move the steam release handle to sealing, select manual, toggle the pressure button to low pressure, and set for 4 minutes. Use a quick release once done.

Remove the lid and then simmer (use the sauté function, adjusting to less heat). Stir in the nutritional yeast and vegan mozzarella. Prop the lid over the pot (do not seal or lock into place) and simmer for about 3 minutes, stirring frequently to avoid sticking.

Serve with chopped fresh cilantro (if using).

Yield: 4 servings

Recipe Note

For an Italian-style variation, use TVP and rehydrate with warm water mixed with dried oregano, parsley, and basil, and opt for canned diced tomatoes with basil and oregano.

Sweet Red Lentil Coconut Curry

I have a client who once told me, "rice is cake." I loved her unabashed testament to loving the white stuff. Together she and I came up with a list of ingredients she loved and created a recipe with many of the same ingredients in the recipe below. In this one, however, I use sushi rice to sweeten the pot and I highly recommend you find some frozen glazed onions, which are more ubiquitous than you might think. If you can't find them though, take some time to quickly caramelize a small onion with a pinch of sugar (method on page 27).

1 teaspoon sesame oil

2 cubes frozen glazed onions

2 large cloves garlic, minced

1 large sweet potato, diced
(about 3 ½ cups, or 385 g)

1/4 cup (60 ml) water

2 tablespoons (35 g) Gochujang
(or other) chili paste

1 teaspoon curry powder

¼ cup (50 g) dried red lentils

½ cup (100 g) sushi rice

1 can (13.5 ounces, or 378 g)
full-fat coconut milk

½ cup (120 ml) vegetable broth

1 teaspoon tamari or soy sauce

½ cup (72 g) chopped unsalted
roasted peanuts, for garnish

¼ cup (4 g) chopped fresh
cilantro, for garnish

Heat the sesame oil in an uncovered Instant Pot or multicooker on the sauté function (adjust to more heat) with the onions, garlic, sweet potatoes, and water for 5 minutes. Add the chili paste, curry powder, lentils, sushi rice, coconut milk, and vegetable broth. Stir well. Cover the pot, move the steam release handle to sealing, select manual (high pressure), and set for 7 minutes. Once done, allow for natural release (release after 10 minutes).

Remove the lid. Begin stirring and you will notice that the sweet potatoes simply melt. Good! Keep stirring until that potatoes have disappeared, turning into a bright cream clinging to the rice. Stir in the tamari.

Spoon into bowls and garnish each serving with peanuts and cilantro.

Yield: 4 to 6 servings

Seitan Swiss Steak

Swiss steak made the dinner rotation when I was growing up.

I often tell people that going vegan doesn't mean we no longer like what we used to eat—we just want a healthier, more compassionate choice. This recipe really grabs all of the elements I recall: the smell of the browning food, the thickness of the tomato gravy, and the need to eat it with mashed potatoes.

3 heaping tablespoons (24 g) flour

1 teaspoon salt

1/4 teaspoon black pepper

4 seitan cutlets (page 174) or 1 package (8 ounces, or 224 g) prepared seitan strips

1/4 cup (60 ml) extra-virgin olive oil

1 cup (160 g) half-moon slices yellow onion

1/2 cup (60 g) chopped celery

1 can (15 ounces, or 420 g) diced tomatoes

1/2 teaspoon vegan Worcestershire sauce

Mix the flour, salt, and pepper on a plate and dredge both sides of each seitan cutlet in the flour. Set aside.

In an uncovered pressure cooker, heat the oil on medium-high. Add the floured seitan and brown for 2 1/2 minutes, then turn over and brown for another 2 1/2 minutes. Transfer the browned seitan to a plate and set aside.

Add 1 tablespoon (8 g) leftover flour mix to the oil and seitan drippings remaining in the pressure cooker. Whisk until thickened. Add the onion, celery, tomatoes, and Worcestershire sauce. This should bubble from the heat right away. Stir well. Place the browned seitan back into the pressure cooker. Gently spoon the tomato gravy over the cutlets.

Cover and bring to pressure. Cook at high pressure for 2 minutes. Use a quick release. Remove the lid and serve immediately.

Yield: 4 servings

Recipe Note

Traditional Worcestershire sauce contains anchovies; if you cannot find a vegan version, substitute with steak sauce mixed with a little soy sauce to thin it out.

Tofu Scramble

Why, you ask? Why make a tofu scramble in the pressure cooker

when you can make it in a skillet fairly quickly? One word: lazy. If you want to get everything going, walk away, and just come back to eat, this one's for you!

¾ cup (180 ml) vegetable broth, divided

3 carrots, diced

2 stalks celery, chopped

½ cup (80 g) diced yellow onion

1 block (14 ounces, or 392 g) firm or extra-firm tofu, pressed and drained

1 teaspoon turmeric

½ teaspoon garlic salt

½ teaspoon chili powder

2 cups (140 g) tightly packed bite-size pieces kale

½ teaspoon sea salt (optional)

In an uncovered pressure cooker, heat ½ cup (120 ml) of the vegetable broth on medium-high. Add the carrots, celery, and onion and sauté until most of the vegetable broth is absorbed, about 3 minutes.

Crumble the tofu with your hands into the pressure cooker. You want the tofu texture to resemble scrambled eggs. Add the turmeric, garlic salt, and chili powder and stir well. Stir in the kale. Pour the remaining ¼ cup (60 ml) vegetable broth over the scramble.

Cover and bring to pressure. Cook at high pressure for 4 minutes. Use a quick release.

Remove the lid, stir in the salt to taste, and serve.

Yield: 4 servings

CHAPTER FIVE

Meal Helpers and Veggie Sides

By now you see that the pressure cooker is great for making bean and grain staples, soups and stews, and one-pot meals. It's a terrific tool to help get quick meals on the table. The recipes in this chapter range from meal helpers to side dishes to make your time in the kitchen quick and delicious.

Rosemary and Thyme Brussels Sprouts, page 132

Turnips and Tomatoes over Freekeh, page 133

Almond Garlic Green Beans, page 134

Lemony Artichokes with Horseradish Butter, page 136

Steamed Kabocha Squash, page 137

Bok Choy, Mushroom, and Onion with Tamari Lime Dressing, page 138

Root Veggie Tagine, page 140

Veggie Stewed Tomatoes, page 142

Instant POT-ato Salad, page 143

"Baked" Sweet Potatoes, page 143

Garlicky Kale and Potatoes, page 144

Mashed Peas and Potatoes, page 146

Shepherd's Pie, page 148

Mashed Sweet Potatoes, page 150

Savory Root Vegetable Mash, page 151

Holiday Roast and Mashed Vegetables, page 152

Vegan "Loose Meat" Sandwiches, page 154

Pulled Jackfruit Sandwiches, page 156

Pinquito Bean Burger, page 157

Vegan Buffalo Wings, page 160

Jackfruit and Sweet Potato Enchiladas, page 163

Tempeh Tacos or Tostadas, page 164

Italian Soybean Balls and Tomato Sauce, page 166

Fiesta Soy Curl and Rice Casserole, page 168

Refried Beans, page 170

White Beans and Rice, page 171

Mediterranean Beans with Greens, page 172

Basic Seitan, page 174

Seitan-Stuffed Acorn Squash, page 175

Vegan Pepperoni "Sausage," page 176

Rosemary and Thyme
Brussels Sprouts

Brussels sprouts are quite possible one of my favorite vegetables—they are delicious and they are a terrific source of calcium and magnesium, which are great for bone health. I opt for the pressure cooker when I don't have the time (or patience) to roast my beloved sprouts.

1 pound (454 g) Brussels sprouts

1 teaspoon whole rosemary leaves

1 teaspoon dried thyme leaves

1 tablespoon (15 ml) walnut oil

1 tablespoon (10 g) coarsely chopped garlic

1/4 teaspoon sea salt

1 cup (235 ml) water

1 teaspoon balsamic vinegar (optional)

Wash the brussels sprouts and remove the stems with a knife; the loose outer leaves should come off easily. Cut each in half. Set aside.

Crumble the rosemary and thyme with a mortar and pestle or by rubbing between you thumb and forefinger. Set aside.

In an uncovered pressure cooker, heat the oil on medium-high. Add the garlic and stir, coating with oil. Add the Brussels sprouts and sauté on medium heat for 5 minutes, stirring frequently. The sprouts will begin to turn a light brown (add a teaspoon or two of water if the garlic or sprouts stick to the pan). Add the rosemary, thyme, salt, and water.

Cover and bring to pressure. Cook at high pressure for 1 minute. Use a quick release.

Remove the lid, stir in the balsamic vinegar, and serve immediately.

Yield: 4 servings

Recipe Note

Substitute extra-virgin olive oil or 1/4 cup (60 ml) vegetable broth for the walnut oil.

Turnips and Tomatoes
over Freekeh

Many people turn their nose up to turnips because they find the taste bitter and—most likely—because they just haven't had them prepared well. Combining tomatoes and maple syrup with turnips makes for a tangy and sweet taste that complements a hearty grain, such as freekeh (see page 40).

1 teaspoon extra-virgin olive oil

1 cup (160 g) diced onion

1 1/2 tablespoons (15 g) minced garlic

4 cups (600 g) peeled and diced turnip

3 cups (540 g) diced fresh tomato

1 tablespoon (8 g) freshly grated ginger

1 teaspoon ground cardamom

1 teaspoon ground coriander

1 teaspoon ground cumin

1/2 teaspoon turmeric powder

1 tablespoon (15 ml) maple syrup

1 tablespoon (15 ml) lime juice

1 cup (235 ml) vegetable broth

1/2 teaspoon sea salt

1 recipe Freekeh, (see page 40)

Add all the ingredients except the salt to the pressure cooker. Cover and bring to pressure. Cook at high pressure for 10 minutes. Use a quick release. Remove the cover, stir in the salt, and serve over the freekeh.

Yield: 4 servings

Almond Garlic Green Beans

I took one of my favorite ways to prepare vegetables—stir-frying them in a little oil and with lots of garlic—and adapted it to the pressure cooker for a super-fast, flavor-infused steamed dish. When cooking vegetables, remember to use a quick release to avoid a mushy result.

1 teaspoon sesame oil

4 or 5 cloves garlic, thinly sliced lengthwise

1 pound (454 g) green beans, cut into $\frac{1}{2}$-inch (1.3 cm) pieces

$\frac{1}{4}$ cup (60 ml) water

$\frac{1}{4}$ teaspoon sea salt

$\frac{1}{4}$ cup (27 g) almond slivers

In an uncovered pressure cooker, heat the oil on medium. Add the garlic and sauté until soft, about 2 minutes.

Add the green beans and water.

Cover and bring to pressure. Cook at pressure for 1 minute. Use a quick release.

Remove the lid stir in the salt. Add the almond slivers, toss, and serve.

Yield: 4 servings

Recipe Note

Substitute sesame oil with olive oil or $\frac{1}{4}$ cup (60 ml) water or vegetable broth.

Lemony Artichokes
with Horseradish Butter

Artichokes are a vegetable I love, but I usually buy them already cooked in a can or frozen. Enter the pressure cooker! With little preparation beyond trimming, the artichoke cooks up in less than 10 minutes and is ready to chop and add to a salad or to dip in your favorite sauce (mine is below).

2 medium artichokes

Juice of 1 lemon

4 tablespoons (56 g) vegan butter

½ teaspoon horseradish powder

Place a trivet in the pressure cooker, place a steamer basket on top of the trivet, and add enough water to come up to, but not in, the basket. Bring the water to a boil.

While the water heats, trim the base of each artichoke with a knife. If you like, you can also remove the sharp points of the leaves with kitchen shears. Add the artichokes and lemon juice to the pressure cooker.

Cover and bring to pressure. Cook at high pressure for 6 to 8 minutes. Use a quick release.

While the artichokes are cooking, heat the vegan butter in the microwave or in a saucepan. Whisk in the horseradish powder and set aside.

Remove the lid and use tongs to remove the steamer basket. Use the tongs to place the artichokes on a plate. Serve with the horseradish butter by dipping each leaf in the butter and sucking out the artichoke meat.

Yield: 2 servings

Steamed Kabocha Squash

Known as the Japanese pumpkin, kabocha squash is wonderful to have on hand to add to soups, to reheat and mash, and to add to cold salads.

1 kabocha squash

Place a trivet in the pressure cooker, place a steamer basket on top of the trivet, and add enough water to come up to, but not in, the basket. Bring the water to a boil.

Wash the kabocha squash well, as the skin is edible. Cut in half and scoop out the seeds. Place the squash in the steamer basket, cut-side up.

Cover and bring to pressure. Cook at high pressure for 4 minutes. Allow for a natural release; if after 10 minutes the pressure has still not come down fully, manually release.

Serve immediately, store in an airtight container in the refrigerator for 3 to 4 days, or freeze in a sturdy bag for 6 to 8 months.

Yield: 4 servings

Bok Choy, Mushrooms, and Onion with Tamari Lime Dressing

Bok choy, a member of the cabbage family, is packed with vitamins A and C. Cooked up quickly with mushroom and onion, this wholesome side dish—served with an umami (see page 27) dressing—delivers a whole lot of flavor.

FOR VEGETABLES:

5 to 6 cups (450 to 540 g) chopped bok choy

2 1/2 cups (175 g) sliced shiitake, cremini, or maitake mushrooms

1 cup (160 g) half-moon slices onion

1/4 teaspoon salt (optional)

FOR DRESSING:

1/2 cup (120 ml) tamari

1 teaspoon minced garlic

1/2 teaspoon red pepper flakes

2 tablespoons (30 ml) lime juice

To make the vegetables: Place a trivet in the pressure cooker, place a steamer basket on top of the trivet, and add enough water to come up to, but not in, the basket. Bring the water to a boil. Place the bok choy, mushrooms, and onion in the basket. Sprinkle a pinch of salt over the vegetables if you are not planning on serving with the dressing.

Cover and bring to pressure. Cook at low pressure for 5 minutes. Use a quick release.

Remove the lid, use tongs to remove the steamer basket, and carefully spoon the vegetables into a bowl.

To make the dressing: Whisk the dressing ingredients together in a bowl. Pour over the vegetables in the bowl, toss lightly, and serve immediately.

Yield: 4 servings

Root Veggie Tagine

Tagine is a North African stew, typically made of spiced meat and
vegetables in a shallow cooking dish. No meat here, and my cooking dish is the pressure cooker.
This dish is packed with spices and flavor. Serve it with the Cinnamon-Curried Chickpeas on
page 25 and couscous or other grains such as barley or freekeh for a rich meal.

2 cups (220 g) diced sweet potatoes (½-inch, or 1.3 cm cubes)

2 cups (240 g) diced carrots
(½-inch, or 1.3 cm)

1 cup (150 g) cubed turnips
(½-inch, or 1.3 cm)

½ teaspoon ground ginger

½ teaspoon ground cumin

½ teaspoon ground cinnamon

½ teaspoon saffron strands

1 teaspoon sugar

½ cup (120 ml) orange juice

½ cup (120 ml) water

½ teaspoon sea salt

Place all the ingredients in the pressure cooker. Stir well,
covering the vegetables with the orange juice and water.
Cover and bring to pressure. Cook at high pressure for
3 to 4 minutes. Use a quick release. Remove the lid, stir,
and serve.

Yield: 4 to 6 servings

Veggie Stewed Tomatoes

This is a great staple to keep in the refrigerator or freezer to add to dishes that require diced or stewed tomatoes. I mix these with cooked elbow macaroni for a Midwestern-style goulash or use them to top a bowl of cooked beans, greens, and grains.

1 tablespoon (15 ml) olive oil

2 cloves garlic, minced

1 cup (160 g) diced onion

½ cup (65 g) chopped carrot

½ cup (60 g) chopped celery

4 cups (600 g) quartered tomatoes

1 tablespoon (2 g) dried basil

1 tablespoon (3 g) dried oregano

1 tablespoon (1.5 g) dried parsley

1 teaspoon red pepper flakes

1 teaspoon salt

½ cup (120 ml) water

2 to 3 tablespoons (32 to 48 g) tomato paste (optional)

Ground black pepper

In an uncovered pressure cooker, heat the oil on medium-high. Add the garlic, onion, carrot, and celery and sauté for about 3 minutes, until the onion is soft. Add the tomatoes, basil, oregano, parsley, red pepper flakes, salt, and water and mix well.

Cover and bring to pressure. Cook at high pressure for 5 minutes. Use a quick release.

Remove the lid. With a potato masher, crush the tomatoes. If a thicker consistency is desired, stir in the tomato paste and simmer, uncovered, for about 5 minutes. Add the ground black pepper to taste.

Yield: 4 cups (980 g)

Recipe Note

These tomatoes keep well in the fridge in an airtight container (try a large mason jar) for a week, or in the freezer in a sturdy plastic bag for 2 to 3 months.

Instant POT-ato Salad

Quick-cooking and delicious!

3 large potatoes, cubed (3 ½ to 4 cups, or 385 to 440 g)

Pinch of salt

2 small green tomatoes, diced (about 2 cups, or 360 g)

1 purple bell pepper or other bell pepper, diced (about 1 cup, or 150 g)

2 teaspoons (6 g) finely diced hot pepper (Pueblo, Anaheim, or Serrano peppers)

1 cup (160 g) chopped red onion

¼ cup (60 g) vegan mayonnaise

2 tablespoons (30 ml) rice vinegar

¼ teaspoon ground black pepper

Heat 1 cup (235 ml) of water in an uncovered Instant Pot or multicooker on the sauté function (adjust to more heat) for 5 minutes. Place a trivet in the Instant Pot and place a steam basket on the trivet. Add the potatoes and a pinch or two of salt. Cover the pot, move the steam release handle to sealing, select the manual function (high pressure), and set for 3 minutes. Once done, allow for a natural release (release after 10 minutes).

Once potatoes are cooled to lukewarm, toss with the remaining ingredients in a large bowl. Refrigerate for a couple of hours, or overnight, before serving.

Yield: 6 to 8 servings

"Baked" Sweet Potatoes

If you love an oven-baked potato

but don't love the wait—and try to avoid the quicker microwave method—this is a nice compromise. In just 18 minutes you'll have a perfectly done potato that you can slice and stuff with your favorite filling. Try it with the Chili-Style Kidney Beans on page 29.

2 cups (470 ml) water

2 medium sweet potatoes

Add the water to the pressure cooker. Insert a rack in the pressure cooker that will keep the potatoes well above the water. Put the potatoes on the rack. Cover and bring to pressure. Cook at high pressure for 18 minutes. Allow for a natural release. Remove the lid and pierce the potatoes with a fork to check for doneness. If not cooked through, bring back to pressure for 3 to 5 minutes and use a quick release.

Yield: 2 servings

Garlicky Kale and Potatoes

Lots of people love to double up foods in their Instant Pot or multicooker—by cooking some food directly in the pot and then adding a second layer with a trivet and/or steam basket. I love doing this for potatoes and veggies as it takes care of two side dishes at once. This is particularly good with seitan (page 174) and gravy (page 182). Special treat for those of you who have my book *The Vegan Air Fryer*: use this method and you can immediately roll the kale and potatoes into balls to make the Kale and Potato Nuggets!

½ cup (120 ml) vegetable broth

3 cloves garlic, minced

2 medium russet potatoes, diced (about 2 cups, or 220 g), or other favorite mashing potato

4 cups (280 g) loosely packed chopped kale

1 tablespoon (15 ml) almond or other plant-based milk

Salt, to taste (optional)

Ground black pepper, to taste (optional)

Heat vegetable broth and garlic in the Instant Pot or multicooker on sauté (adjust to less heat) for 3 minutes. Add the potatoes. Place a trivet over the potatoes and set a steamer basket on top. Add the kale to the steamer basket.

Cover the pot, move the steam release handle to sealing, select manual, toggle the pressure button to low pressure, and set to 7 minutes. Use a quick release once done.

Remove the cover and pull the steam basket with the kale out of the pot with tongs or silicone gloves. Set aside. Add the almond milk, salt, and pepper to the potatoes, and mash with a hand masher. If there's too much liquid, set the Instant Pot on sauté, adjust to less heat, and mash until the liquid is absorbed. Transfer the cooked kale into the pot and stir to combine.

Yield: 4 servings

Mashed Peas and Potatoes

A colorful, quick mash, these bright green peas, a legume, pack a whopping 8 grams of protein. That means you can have this mashed potato dish as an entrée—guilt-free!

Salt

2 pounds (908 g) butter cream potatoes (or other small, new potatoes)

8 ounces (228 g) English peas, shelled

1/2 cup (120 ml) almond milk

2 tablespoons (28 g) vegan butter

1/4 teaspoon thyme leaves

1/4 teaspoon whole rosemary

Place a trivet in the pressure cooker, place a steamer basket on top of the trivet, and add enough water to come up to, but not in, the basket. Add a pinch of salt. Bring the water to a boil.

Scrub the potatoes (leave the skin on) and rinse the English peas. Place the potatoes in the steamer basket. Pour the peas over the potatoes.

Cover and bring to pressure. Cook at high pressure for 6 minutes. Use a quick release.

Uncover the pressure cooker and gently remove the steamer basket with kitchen tongs. Pour any remaining water out of the pressure cooker. Transfer the potatoes and peas back into the pressure cooker (alternatively, you can use a large bowl). Add the almond milk and butter. Mash with a potato masher to make this nice and chunky. Crumble the thyme leaves and whole rosemary with a mortar and pestle or by rubbing between your fingers and thumbs and sprinkle over the potatoes and peas and stir. Add salt to taste.

Yield: 4 servings

Shepherd's Pie

After becoming a whiz with mashed veggies in the pressure cooker, it was just a matter of time before I tried my hand at a vegan shepherd's pie. This recipe calls for cooked lentils; to save time, make them up to two days in advance and store in an airtight container in the refrigerator.

1 ½ cups (355 ml) water

4 tablespoons (32 g) minced garlic, divided

4 cups (440 g) quartered fingerling potatoes

2 cups (260 g) baby carrots

1 teaspoon sea salt

2 tablespoons (28 g) vegan butter

1 tablespoon (15 ml) extra-virgin olive oil

¾ cup (120 g) diced onion

½ cup (60 g) chopped celery

3 cups (510 g) cooked lentils

1 tablespoon (15 ml) vegan Worcestershire sauce

1 teaspoon ground dried rosemary

1 teaspoon ground dried thyme

4 cups (280 g) loosely packed chopped kale

¼ cup (60 g) creamy vegan mushroom soup

Freshly ground pepper

Preheat the oven to 350°F (180°C, or gas mark 4). Grease a 13 x 7-inch (33 x 18 cm) baking dish.

In an uncovered pressure cooker bring the water to a boil. Add 2 tablespoons (16 g) of the garlic, the potatoes, and the carrots.

Cover and bring to pressure. Cook at high pressure for 6 minutes. Use a quick release.

Remove the lid, add the salt and vegan butter, and mash with a hand masher. Set aside.

Heat the extra-virgin olive oil in a large skillet over medium-high. Sauté the remaining 2 tablespoons (16 g) garlic, the onion, and the celery for about 1 minute. Add the cooked lentils, Worcestershire sauce, rosemary, and thyme and mix well. Add the kale and mushroom soup and let simmer on medium-low for about 5 minutes, stirring frequently.

Pour the lentil and kale filling into the prepared baking dish. Spread the mashed carrots and potatoes over the top of the filling. Season with pepper to taste. Transfer to the oven and bake until bubbling and golden, about 30 minutes.

Cool slightly on a wire rack for at least 5 minutes before serving (this helps the pie set).

Yield: 8 to 10 servings

Recipe Note

Remember, traditional Worcestershire contains anchovies—not vegan—so you'll want a vegan brand.

Mashed Sweet Potatoes

One of my favorite side dishes is mashed anything. Well, mashed root vegetables. I stumbled on this when spying a potato that was on the edge of use it or lose it. So I tossed it in the pressure cooker, directly into the vegetable broth, and after 6 minutes at pressure and a quick release it was perfect for mashing. I soon discovered I could mix a variety of vegetables for a quick mash.

2 large sweet potatoes, quartered

A splash of almond milk or other nondairy milk

2 teaspoons vegan butter, divided

Pinch of salt

Place a trivet in the pressure cooker, place a steamer basket on top of the trivet, and add enough water to come up to, but not in, the basket. Bring the water to a boil. Place the potatoes in the basket.

Cover and bring to pressure. Cook at high pressure for 6 minutes. Allow for a natural release.

Remove the lid and transfer the potatoes to a bowl. Remove the peel from the potatoes (the skin on the potatoes will peel off with no effort at all). Add a splash of almond milk, 1 teaspoon vegan butter, and salt. Mash with a potato masher. Serve with the remaining 1 teaspoon butter.

Yield: 4 servings

Savory Root Vegetable Mash

I'm partial to root vegetables in the pressure cooker because they are so good for you and so delicious, but they often require a longer cook time, whether boiling or roasting. You can use any root vegetable that you like in this recipe.

4 carrots, cut into 2-inch (5 cm) pieces

5 or 6 whole baby turnips

2 cups (220 g) halved fingerling potatoes

2 cloves garlic, peeled but whole

½ teaspoon dried herbes de Provence

¼ cup (60 ml) unsweetened almond milk

¼ teaspoon sea salt (optional)

Freshly ground black pepper

Place a trivet in the pressure cooker, place a steamer basket on top of the trivet, and add enough water to come up to, but not in, the basket. Bring the water to a boil. Place the carrots, turnips, potatoes, and garlic in the steamer basket.

Cover and bring to pressure. Cook at high pressure for 6 minutes. Use a quick release.

Remove the lid, carefully remove the steamer basket with tongs, and transfer the vegetables to a large bowl. Add the herbes de Provence, almond milk, salt, and pepper to taste and mash with a hand masher. Serve immediately.

Yield: 6 servings

Recipe Note

When making mashed potatoes and other root vegetables:

- You can always substitute plant milk for coconut oil for creaminess.

- Use vegetable broth if you want a lower fat version.

- Stir in a little maple syrup for added sweetness.

- To add an umami element, stir in caramelized onions after mashing.

Holiday Roast
with Mashed Vegetables

Times are changing. You can now find vegan stuffed roasts in grocery stores during the holiday season! I have baked and slow cooked a few, but I find pressure cooking the best way to prepare these dense, precooked roasts; the outcome is a soft, succulent dish.

1 to 2 teaspoons extra-virgin olive oil

4 cloves garlic, minced

1 cup (160 g) diced yellow onion

2 cups (260 g) diced carrot

2 cups (220 g) diced potato

1 teaspoon sea salt

1 vegan stuffed roast (1 pound, or 454 g), thawed

3/4 to 1 cup (180 to 235 ml) vegetable broth

1 tablespoon (15 ml) almond milk

1/4 teaspoon ground black pepper

1 teaspoon vegan butter (optional)

In an uncovered pressure cooker, heat the oil on medium-high. Add the garlic and onion and sauté for 1 minute. Add the carrots, potatoes, and salt. Mix well. Place the thawed roast on top of the vegetables and pour the vegetable broth over the roast.

Cover and bring to pressure. Cook at low pressure for 8 minutes. Use a quick release.

Remove the lid, remove the roast, and set aside.

Add the almond milk, black pepper, and vegan butter to the vegetables in the pressure cooker and mash with a potato masher. Slice the roast and serve with the mashed vegetables.

Yield: 4 servings

Recipe Note

If you're using a multifunction electric pressure cooker, you can also use the slow-cooking function for 1 hour.

Vegan "Loose Meat" Sandwiches

Not a sloppy Joe and not quite a Maid-Rite, this is a vegan version of a loose meat sandwich that is oh so simple and tasty! This filling is terrific served on a toasted bun with yellow mustard and onions. I have also used it for hard-shell tacos.

2 tablespoons (28 g) vegan butter

½ cup (80 g) diced onion

1 cup (70 g) diced mushrooms

½ teaspoon cumin

½ teaspoon garlic powder

¼ teaspoon sea salt, or more as needed

¼ teaspoon liquid smoke

½ cup (120 ml) almond milk

1 cup (100 g) TVP

½ cup (120 ml) vegetable broth

½ teaspoon ground black pepper

4 hamburger buns, toasted

In an uncovered pressure cooker, heat the butter on medium-high. Add the onion and mushrooms and sauté for 3 minutes, until the onion softens. Add the seasonings and almond milk and bring to a light boil. Add the TVP and vegetable broth and stir well.

Cover and bring to pressure. Cook at high pressure for 3 minutes. Use a quick release.

Remove the lid, stir in the pepper, and add more salt, if needed. Spoon onto the hamburger buns.

Yield: 4 sandwiches

Pulled Jackfruit Sandwiches

Jackfruit is, well, a fruit. Its flesh is very meaty and, when cooked, it shreds, so it's become a darling among vegans who want to mimic shredded meat recipes.

1 teaspoon extra-virgin olive oil

¼ cup (40 g) finely diced onion

1 tablespoon (8 g) minced garlic

1 can (17 ounces, or 476 g) jackfruit, packed in water, rinsed and drained

½ teaspoon cayenne pepper

½ teaspoon yellow mustard seeds

½ teaspoon ground black pepper

½ teaspoon salt, or to taste

3 tablespoons (48 g) tomato paste

1 teaspoon apple cider vinegar

1 teaspoon vegan Worcestershire sauce

1 tablespoon (15 ml) maple, date, or brown rice syrup

½ to ¾ cup (120 to 180 ml) water

4 buns, toasted

In an uncovered pressure cooker heat the oil on medium-high. Add the onion and garlic and sauté for 3 minutes, until the onion is soft. Add the jackfruit, seasonings, tomato paste, vinegar, Worcestershire, and syrup and stir to combine. Add enough of the water to cover the jackfruit and mix well.

Cover and bring to pressure. Cook at high pressure for 3 minutes. Allow for a natural release.

Remove the lid and stir the jackfruit and sauce well. Use a fork to pull the jackfruit into shreds. This should be very easy to do. Serve on the toasted buns.

Yield: 4 servings

Recipe Notes

• Canned jackfruit is often packed in syrup or sugar water and you do not want this! Look for the type that's packed in water or brine. Both varieties are most commonly found at Asian markets, but if you don't have one, try an online store.

• Remember, traditional Worcestershire contains anchovies—not vegan—so you'll want a vegan brand.

Pinquito Bean Burger

An heirloom bean, Pinquito beans are a cousin to the pinto. They
are pretty special so try to find them, but feel free to use dried pinto beans if you can't.

FOR BEANS:

1 cup (200 g) dried Pinquito (or
  pinto beans), soaked overnight

3 cups (705 ml) water

FOR SPELT BERRIES:

1 cup (174 g) dried spelt berries

3 cups (705 ml) water

Pinch of salt

FOR BURGERS:

1 1/2 cups (360 g) cooked Pinquito
  (or cooked/canned pinto) beans

1/2 cup (97 g) cooked spelt berries

2 tablespoons (18 g) diced
  jalapeño

1 teaspoon chili powder

1/2 teaspoon sea salt

1/4 teaspoon black pepper

1 cup (160 g) diced onion

1 cup (150 g) diced red bell
  pepper

1 cup (130 g) diced carrots

2 tablespoons (10 g) dry
  VeganEgg

1/4 cup plus 2 tablespoons (90 ml)
  very cold water

1 cup (80 g) old-fashioned oats

1/2 teaspoon dried hickory smoke
  powder

To make the beans: Rinse and drain the beans. Combine
the beans and water in the Instant Pot or multicooker.
Cover the pot, move the steam release handle to sealing,
select manual (high pressure), and set for 6 minutes.
Once done, allow for a natural release.

Transfer the beans and broth to an airtight container.
Allow to cool at room temperature for 1 to 2 hours before storing in the refrigerator or freezer. (If refrigerated,
consume within 3 to 5 days; freeze for 3 months.)

To make the spelt berries: Combine the spelt berries
and water in the Instant Pot or multicooker. Add a pinch
of salt. Cover the pot, move the steam release handle
to sealing, select manual (high pressure), and set for
15 minutes. Once done, allow for a natural release.

Drain the spelt berries before transferring to an airtight container. Allow to cool at room temperature for
1 to 2 hours before storing in the refrigerator or freezer.
(If refrigerated, consume within 3 to 5 days; freeze for
3 months.)

To make the burgers: Add the cooked beans, spelt,
diced jalapeño, chili powder, salt, and pepper to a food
processor. Quickly pulse (10 seconds or so). Add the
onion, red pepper, and carrots. Quickly pulse; you want
some veggie chunks, so don't over process! Transfer to a
large mixing bowl.

Whisk VeganEgg mix with cold water, then add to the
mixing bowl and stir. Fold in the oats and dry hickory
smoke. Mix well.

Form patties (about 1/2 cup each), and place on dish
or in a container (separate layers of burgers with parchment paper or foil). Refrigerate 4 hours (or overnight).

continued on next page

continued from previous page

Set burgers out about 30 minutes before baking and heat oven to 400°F (200°C, or gas mark 6).

Bake on a large cast iron skillet sprayed with vegetable oil, for 30 to 40 minutes, flipping halfway through, until lightly browned.

Yield: 8 patties

Recipe Notes

- You can make these patties in an air fryer! Cook on 375°F (190°C) for 15 to 20 minutes, flipping halfway through.

- Rye or wheat berries are a fine substitute. Cooking time ranges from 25 minutes to 30 minutes, respectively.

- Make-ahead tip: prepare the beans and spelt berries during a weekend bulk-cooking session and then use them later in the week to make these burgers, sides, and more.

Vegan Buffalo Wings

The seitan recipes in this book have been reader favorites so I couldn't help but share the recipe that my husband and I now make *all the time*. Game day, picnics, potlucks, or just the two of us for dinner, these vegan wings are versatile! Serve as a snack with celery or make a vegan Caesar salad and serve the wings over it.

FOR SEITAN:

1 1/2 cups (180 g) vital wheat gluten

1/4 cup (30 g) chickpea flour

2 tablespoons (14 g) nutritional yeast

1 1/2 teaspoon chicken-style vegan seasoning or bouillon powder

1/2 teaspoon garlic powder

1/2 teaspoon fresh ground black pepper

1 cup (235 ml) chicken-style vegetable broth (make with granules or use shelf-stable not-chicken broth)

1 teaspoon extra-virgin olive oil

1 teaspoon blackstrap molasses

2 tablespoons (30 ml) low-sodium tamari sauce

FOR COOKING BROTH:

3 cups (705 ml) water

3 cups (705 ml) broth

1/4 cup (60 ml) low-sodium tamari sauce,

1 tablespoon (8 g) chicken-style vegan seasoning or bouillon powder

To make the seitan: Combine the gluten, chickpea flour, nutritional yeast, seasoning, garlic powder, and pepper in a medium bowl or stand mixer.

Whisk together the wet ingredients (NOT the cooking broth) in a small bowl. Transfer the wet ingredients to the bowl with the dry ingredients and stir until well combined.

Knead the seitan dough for 5 minutes by hand or use the dough hook with a stand mixer.

Pull the dough apart to form 6 cutlets. Set aside.

Heat the cooking broth ingredients in an uncovered Instant Pot or multicooker on the sauté function (adjust to more) for about 10 minutes. Add the cutlets to the hot broth. Cover the pot, move the steam release handle to sealing, select the manual function, toggle the pressure button to low pressure, and set for 30 minutes. Once done, allow for a natural release.

Remove the cutlets from the broth and place on a baking rack to cool.

To make the Buffalo sauce: Add the butter to a saucepan and melt over medium-high heat. Add Frank's Hot Sauce and garlic. Stir well and heat on low while preparing the seitan.

To fry the seitan: Slice the seitan into 2-inch by 1-inch (5-cm by 2.5-cm) slices. You'll get about a dozen.

In a bowl, mix the flour and cornmeal. Dredge the seitan pieces into the mix until uniformly coated.

Heat a cast iron skillet on medium-high. Add vegetable oil (enough to cover the bottom of the pan). Brown

continued on next page

FOR BUFFALO SAUCE:

3 tablespoons (42 g) vegan butter

1 cup (235 ml) Frank's Hot Sauce (original)

2 cloves garlic, minced

FOR FRYING:

¼ cup (40 g) flour (we used brown rice flour)

¼ cup (35 g) cornmeal

Vegetable oil, for frying

FOR SERVING:

Celery stalks

Vegan blue cheese or ranch dressing (page 180)

the seitan pieces on both sides (about 2 minutes per side).

Transfer the fried seitan from the skillet to a large bowl. Pour the warm Buffalo sauce over the seitan and toss to coat.

Serve with celery and vegan ranch or blue cheese dressing.

Yield: 6 to 8 servings

Recipe Note

For an Asian-style alternative to the Buffalo sauce, pour 1 cup Asian Hot Sauce (page 181) into a saucepan. Add 2 cloves minced garlic and stir well. Heat on low while frying the seitan and proceed with the rest of the recipe.

Jackfruit and Sweet Potato Enchiladas

Enchiladas are often associated with meat and cheese. Here jackfruit adds the meaty texture and mashed sweet potatoes lend a cheesy consistency, along with a little vegan cheese topping.

FOR JACKFRUIT FILLING:

1 teaspoon extra-virgin olive oil

4 cloves garlic, finely diced

1/4 cup (40 g) diced onion

3/4 cup (83 g) diced sweet potato

1 can (17 ounces, or 476 g) jackfruit, packed in water, rinsed and drained

1 teaspoon ground cumin

2 teaspoons taco seasoning

1 teaspoon chili powder

1/4 teaspoon salt

1/2 to 1 cup (120 to 235 ml) vegetable broth

FOR ENCHILADAS:

1 can (12 ounces, or 336 g) red enchilada sauce

10 to 12 (6-inch, or 15 cm) corn tortillas

1 can (4 ounces, or 112 g) diced green chiles

1 can (2.25 ounces, 63 g) sliced black olives, drained

1 cup (120 g) shredded vegan cheddar cheese, to cover the enchiladas

Preheat the oven to 350°F (180°C, or gas mark 4). Grease a 13 x 7-inch (33 x 18 cm) baking dish.

To make the jackfruit filling: In an uncovered pressure cooker, heat the oil on medium-high. Add the garlic and onion and sauté for 3 minutes, until the onion is soft. Add the sweet potatoes and sauté for another minute or two. Add the jackfruit, cumin, taco seasoning, chili powder, salt, and enough vegetable broth to cover the potatoes and jackfruit. Stir well.

Cover and bring to pressure. Cook at high pressure for 3 minutes. Allow for a natural release.

Remove the lid, stir well, and use your spoon, or a fork, to shred the jackfruit. Set aside.

To make the enchiladas: In a shallow saucepan, heat the enchilada sauce over medium-low heat. Take each tortilla, one by one, and place into the saucepan to coat. Let each tortilla sit in the warm sauce for 20 to 30 seconds (turning once or twice to coat completely). Remove to a plate.

Once all tortillas are done, remove the sauce from heat and set aside. Take 1 tablespoon (15 g) filling and spread in the middle of the tortilla. Add some green chiles and black olive slices (about 1/2 teaspoon each). Fold or roll the tortilla and place in the prepared baking dish, seam-side down. Repeat with remaining tortillas, then pour the remaining sauce over them in the pan. Sprinkle with the cheese and the remaining olives and green chiles. Bake until heated through and bubbling, 20 to 25 minutes.

Yield: 10 to 12 enchiladas

Tempeh Tacos or Tostadas

In this healthy twist on traditional Mexican fare, tempeh—a soy–based powerhouse packed with fiber, calcium, iron, vitamin B-6, and over 60 percent of USDA daily protein recommendations—offers a meaty texture that is 100 percent plant-based.

FOR TEMPEH FILLING:

1 package (8 ounces, or 224 g) package tempeh

2 cups (470 ml) vegetable broth, divided

2 cloves garlic, minced

1/2 cup (80 g) diced red onion

1/4 cup (30 g) finely diced celery

2 cups (140 g) diced cremini mushrooms

1 seeded and diced fresh jalapeño

1/2 cup (130 g) mild salsa

1 to 2 teaspoons chili powder

Juice of 1/2 lime

1/2 teaspoon salt

FOR SPINACH:

1 teaspoon extra-virgin olive oil

2 cloves garlic, minced

8 cups (480 g) loosely packed baby spinach

Pinch of salt

Juice of 1/2 lime

6 taco shells or corn tortillas, baked or fried in oil until crispy

1/2 cup (120 g) vegan sour cream

1 lime, cut into 6 wedges

To make the tempeh: Cut tempeh into 4 equal pieces. Add to an uncovered pressure cooker with 1 cup (235 ml) of the vegetable broth. Cover and bring to pressure. As soon as pressure is achieved use a quick release.

Remove the lid and return to medium-high heat. Crumble the tempeh into a "ground meat" consistency with a spoon. Add the garlic, onion, celery, mushrooms, jalapeño, and salsa. Everything will be boiling. Add the chili powder and remaining 1 cup (235 ml) vegetable broth. Stir well.

Cover and return to pressure. Cook at high pressure for 3 minutes. Allow for a natural release. Remove the lid, add the lime juice and salt, and simmer on low to cook off the extra liquid.

To make the spinach: Heat the olive oil in a skillet over medium-high heat. Add the garlic and spinach and sauté for 30 seconds, tossing with tongs to prevent sticking. Add the salt and lime juice, toss, and remove from the heat.

Place a layer of spinach on each of the tacos shells or corn tortillas for tostadas. Add the tempeh and a dollop of sour cream and serve with a wedge of lime.

Yield: 6 servings

Recipe Note

Follow the first step in this recipe *anytime* you are using tempeh! It's a super quick way to steam it, which softens it and prepares it to absorb your marinade of choice.

Italian Soybean Balls and Tomato Sauce

Thanks to a food processor and the pressure cooker, this meal comes together quickly. While the soybean balls are cooking, heat up water in a pan and make your favorite pasta. You'll be enjoying a soybean ball and tomato sauce pasta dish in less than 30 minutes!

FOR SOYBEAN BALLS:

1 cup (200 g) dried black soybeans, soaked for 12 hours or overnight

2 to 3 cups (470 to 705 ml) water plus 6 tablespoons (90 ml) warm water, divided

1 tablespoon (15 ml) vegetable oil

1/2 cup (50 g) TVP

1/2 cup (120 ml) vegetable broth, warm

2 tablespoons (14 g) ground flaxseed

2 tablespoons (16 g) black sesame seeds

2 tablespoons (14 g) Italian herb bread crumbs

1 teaspoon salt

2 tablespoons (14 g) nutritional yeast

2 tablespoons (14 g) Italian seasoning

1/2 teaspoon red pepper flakes

1/2 teaspoon black pepper

To make the soybean balls: Rinse and drain the soaked black soybeans. Add to a pressure cooker with the 2 to 3 cups (470 to 705 ml) water, enough to cover the beans by 2 inches (5 cm), and the oil. Cover and bring to pressure. Cook at high pressure for 20 to 22 minutes—opt for the lower cooking time here to give the beans a bit of a "crunch" as they will continue cooking when the soybean balls are cooked with the sauce. Allow for a natural release; if after 10 minutes the pressure has still not come down fully, manually release.

Meanwhile, soak the TVP in the warm vegetable broth in a bowl for 10 minutes.

Prepare the flax egg by whisking the ground flaxseed in the remaining 6 tablespoons (90 ml) warm water and let sit for 10 minutes.

Pulse the black soybeans, TVP, flax egg, sesame seeds, bread crumbs, salt, nutritional yeast, Italian seasoning, red pepper flakes, and black pepper in a food processor for 15 seconds, long enough to mix well but avoid liquefying or making too creamy.

Make soybean balls by scooping out 2 to 3 tablespoons (28 to 42 g) and rolling in your hands. You should get about 36 balls. Set the soybean balls aside.

FOR SAUCE:

1 tablespoon (15 ml)
    vegetable oil

3 cloves garlic, minced

1 cup (160 g) diced red onion

1/2 cup (75 g) diced green
    bell pepper

1/2 cup (75 g) diced red
    bell pepper

1 cup (130 g) diced carrot

1 can (15 ounces, or 425 g)
    tomato sauce

1 1/2 cup (354 ml) vegetable
    broth

2 tablespoons (14 g) Italian
    seasoning

1/2 teaspoon black pepper

Cooked pasta of choice

To make the sauce: In an uncovered pressure cooker heat the oil on medium-high. Add the garlic, onion, peppers, and carrots and sauté, stirring frequently, for 5 minutes. If necessary, add water to avoid sticking. Stir in the tomato sauce, broth, Italian seasoning, and black pepper. Gingerly place the soybean balls in the sauce.

Cover and bring to pressure. Cook at low pressure for 2 minutes. Use a quick release.

Remove the lid. Spoon over the cooked pasta.

Yield: 4 servings; 36 soybean balls

Recipe Notes

- I make soybean balls all the time. Sometimes they come out as perfect, round balls and sometimes they come apart a bit. When that happens I just stir vigorously and turn it into soy-meat sauce—we love it that way, too!

- You can make the black beans 2 or 3 days in advance and store in an airtight container in the refrigerator.

- If you want to skip the oil in the sauce, substitute 1/4 cup (60 ml) water or vegetable broth.

- If you don't have Italian herb bread crumbs, substitute whatever type you have (or make your own!).

Fiesta Soy Curl and Rice Casserole

Soy curls are a great substitute for traditional chicken dishes.

Made from the whole soybean, they are packed with protein and extremely versatile. A loose casserole, this is best served in a bowl. For a fun treat, serve it on top of blue or yellow corn tortilla chips and enjoy a hearty plate of nachos for lunch or dinner.

3 cups (300 g) soy curls

4 cups (940 ml) vegetable broth, warm, divided

1 teaspoon extra-virgin olive oil

2 cloves garlic, minced

1/2 cup (80 g) diced yellow onion

2 tablespoons (16 g) vegan chicken-flavored seasoning

1 tablespoon (8 g) taco seasoning

1 cup (190 g) long-grain white rice

1 can (15.25-ounce, or 427 g) corn, drained

1 can (28 ounces, or 784 g) diced tomatoes with green chiles

1 can (8 ounces, or 224 g) tomato sauce

1/2 to 1 teaspoon sea salt

1 1/2 cups (180 g) shredded vegan cheese, divided

1 cup (70 g) crumbled corn tortilla chips

Freshly ground black pepper

Preheat the oven to 375°F (190°C, or gas mark 5). Grease a 13 x 7-inch (33 x 18 cm) casserole dish.

Soak the soy curls in 3 cups (705 ml) of the warm vegetable broth in a bowl for 15 minutes. Drain the soy curls and set aside.

In an uncovered pressure cooker, heat the olive oil on medium-high. Add the garlic and onion and sauté for 3 minutes, until the onion is soft. Add the drained soy curls, chicken-flavored seasoning, and taco seasoning and sauté for 3 to 5 minutes. Note: Soy curls, much like tofu, need time to absorb the flavors. Add water or vegetable broth if they begin to stick to the pan. Add the rice, corn, tomatoes and chiles, tomato sauce, and remaining 1 cup (235 ml) vegetable broth and mix well.

Cover and bring to pressure. Cook at high pressure for 4 minutes. Use a quick release.

Remove the lid. Taste and add salt as needed. Stir in 1 cup (120 g) of the shredded vegan cheese. Transfer to the prepared casserole dish.

In a small bow, mix the remaining 1/2 cup (60 g) shredded vegan cheese with the crumbled tortilla chips. Sprinkle over the casserole.

Bake for 10 minutes, or until the cheese is melted. Serve with freshly ground black pepper.

Yield: 8 to 10 servings

Refried Beans

These beans are great as a side dish when making a full Mexican dinner but you can also use them as the filling for tacos or on top of vegan nachos as an entrée. I love to spread them on a whole-wheat tortilla with chopped lettuce, shredded vegan cheddar cheese, and a dollop of sour cream for a Mexican-style wrap sandwich.

1 cup (200 g) dried pinto beans, soaked for 12 hours or overnight

1 tablespoon (15 ml) extra-virgin olive oil

½ cup (80 g) diced yellow onion

4 cloves garlic, minced

1 or 2 seeded and diced fresh jalapeños

2 to 3 cups (470 to 705 ml) water or vegetable broth

1 teaspoon chili powder

½ teaspoon cumin

¼ teaspoon cayenne pepper

½ to 1 teaspoon salt

Rinse and drain the beans.

In an uncovered pressure cooker, heat the oil on medium-high. Add the onion, garlic, and jalapeño and sauté for 3 minutes, until the onion is soft. Add the pinto beans and enough water or vegetable broth to cover the beans plus another 1 inch (2.5 cm) of liquid. Add the chili powder, cumin, and cayenne pepper. Stir to combine.

Cover and bring to pressure. Cook for 6 minutes at high pressure. Allow for a natural release.

Remove the lid, drain the beans (reserve the liquid in a measure cup) and return the beans to the pressure cooker. Add salt to taste. Begin mashing the beans with a hand masher. For a creamier refried beans, add some of the cooking liquid as needed.

Yield: 4 to 6 servings

White Beans and Rice

A vegan twist on traditional red beans and rice with sausage, this dish uses white beans, brown rice, and vegan pepperoni. This is a meal helper because you can make the beans, rice, and even homemade pepperoni (page 177) anytime and bring them together for this meal.

1 cup (200 g) dried navy beans, soaked for 12 hours or overnight

1 teaspoon extra-virgin olive oil

1/2 cup (80 g) diced sweet onion

2 cloves garlic, minced

1/2 teaspoon cayenne pepper

1 bay leaf

2 to 3 cups (470 to 705 ml) vegetable broth

1 1/2 cups (262 g) cubed vegan pepperoni sausage, homemade (page 149) or store-bought

1/2 teaspoon salt, or to taste

3 cups (480 g) cooked brown rice, for serving

Rinse and drain the beans.

In an uncovered pressure cooker, heat the oil on medium-high. Add the onion and garlic and sauté for 2 to 3 minutes, until softened. Add the cayenne pepper, bay leaf, and beans. Stir in the vegetable broth to cover, plus another 1 inch (2.5 cm) of liquid. Stir to combine.

Cover and bring to pressure. Cook at high pressure for 6 to 8 minutes. Allow for a natural release.

Remove the lid. Stir in the pepperoni sausage and let simmer, uncovered, for a few minutes to heat the sausage through. Taste and season with salt, if needed. Serve over the brown rice.

Yield: 4 to 6 servings

Mediterranean Beans with Greens

This dish epitomizes the Mediterranean diet—low in saturated fats and high in fiber and other nutrients. Plus, it pleases vegans and omnivores alike! I created a stove top version of this recipe for my book *Vegan for Her*; cooking the beans, tomatoes, and olives together in the pressure cooker intensifies the flavor immensely.

1 cup (200 g) dried navy or cannellini beans, soaked for 12 hours or overnight

2 cups (470 ml) vegetable broth

2 cans (14.5 ounces, or 406 g) cans diced tomatoes with basil, garlic, and oregano

½ cup (50 g) sliced green olives, plus extra for garnish

1 teaspoon extra-virgin olive oil

4 cloves garlic, finely diced

8 cups (140 g) loosely packed arugula (about 5 ounces, or 140 g)

½ cup (120 ml) freshly squeezed lemon juice, divided

Pinch of salt

2 cups (320 g) cooked pearl barley (see page 47)

Rinse and drain the beans.

Add the beans, broth, diced tomatoes, and olives to the pressure cooker. Cover and bring to pressure. Cook at high pressure for 6 to 8 minutes. Allow for a natural release.

While the beans are cooking, heat the olive oil in a skillet over medium-high heat. Add the garlic and sauté until soft but not brown, 1 to 2 minutes. Add the arugula and ¼ cup (60 ml) of the lemon juice to the skillet and, using tongs, turn the arugula frequently for 30 seconds. It will wilt quickly, which is what you want, but remove from the heat before turning brown. Set aside.

Remove the lid from the pressure cooker and stir in the remaining ¼ cup (60 ml) lemon juice. Taste. The olives and tomatoes should be sufficient, but add salt, if desired.

To serve, begin with a plate of cooked pearl barley, add the arugula, and then top with the beans and tomatoes. Add a few olive slices for garnish.

Yield: 4 servings

Recipe Note

To keep this recipe simple, I buy diced tomatoes seasoned with basil, garlic, and oregano. If you opt for a can of plain diced tomatoes, consider adding basil, garlic, and oregano for extra flavor.

Basic Seitan

Seitan, also known as "wheat meat," can take on a variety of flavors simply by changing up the spices and seasoning. Follow this recipe, or swap out the cumin and Italian seasoning for 1 ½ teaspoons of the spices of your choice and you change the flavor but not the texture. This makes a great plant-based dinner, as it is familiar in both taste and texture to meat-based dishes. Chickpea flour is also labeled as garbanzo bean, gram, or besan flour at Asian grocers.

FOR SEITAN:

1½ cups (180 g) vital wheat gluten

¼ cup (30 g) chickpea flour

2 tablespoons (14 g) nutritional yeast

½ teaspoon garlic powder

½ teaspoon ground black pepper

½ teaspoon ground ginger

½ teaspoon ground cinnamon

½ teaspoon ground cumin

1 cup (235 ml) vegetable broth

1 teaspoon avocado oil

1 teaspoon blackstrap molasses

2 tablespoons (30 ml) Bragg Liquid Aminos or soy sauce

FOR BROTH:

3 cups (705 ml) water

3 cups (705 ml) vegetable broth

¼ cup (60 ml) low-sodium soy sauce

To make the seitan: Combine the gluten, chickpea flour, nutritional yeast, and seasonings in a medium bowl or a stand mixer. In a separate bowl, whisk together the broth, oil, molasses, and liquid aminos. Add the wet ingredients to the dry ingredients and stir until well combined.

Knead for 5 minutes, either by hand or using the dough hook of the stand mixer.

Roll the dough into one long log and slice into 6 cutlets. Set aside.

To make the broth: In an uncovered pressure cooker add the broth ingredients and bring to a boil.

Add the cutlets, cover, and bring to pressure. Cook at low pressure for 30 minutes. Remove from the heat and allow for a natural release.

Remove the cutlets from the broth to cool before handling or serving.

Yield: 6 seitan cutlets; 8 to 10 servings

Recipe Note

Store leftover cutlets in the cooking broth in an airtight container in the refrigerator or in a sturdy bag in the freezer.

Seitan-Stuffed Acorn Squash

When I make homemade seitan (page 174), I often crumble a portion and store it, in broth, in the freezer. It's a great substitute for recipes calling for ground meat. You can also find crumbled meat alternatives in the freezer section of many grocery stores.

1 acorn squash

Pinch of sea salt

1 teaspoon extra-virgin olive oil

¼ cup (40 g) chopped onion

¼ cup (30 g) chopped celery

1 cup (110 g) crumbled seitan

1 cup (70 g) diced shiitake mushrooms

½ teaspoon dried sage

¼ teaspoon dried thyme

¼ teaspoon ground black pepper

1 teaspoon Sriracha or your favorite hot sauce

Cut the squash in half and scoop out the seeds. Cut or scoop out enough squash flesh to make room for ½ cup (55 g) of the seitan filling in each cavity—you'll end up with about ¼ cup (40 g) squash flesh: chop and set aside. Sprinkle a little salt over the squash halves and set aside.

In a skillet, heat the olive oil over medium-high heat. Add the onion and celery and sauté until the onion is translucent, 2 to 3 minutes. Add the chopped squash, seitan, mushrooms, sage, thyme, pepper, and Sriracha and stir to combine. Sauté for about 5 minutes, until the seitan is lightly browned. Spoon the sautéed seitan mixture into the 2 squash halves.

Place a trivet in the pressure cooker, place a steamer basket on top of the trivet, and add enough water to come up to, but not in, the basket. Bring the water to a boil. Place the squash in the steamer basket. If the squash halves do not fit in the basket, turn the basket upside down for a flat surface. Place foil loosely over the top of the squash.

Cover and bring to pressure. Cook at pressure for 10 minutes. Use a quick release.

Remove the pressure cooker lid, remove the foil, and let the squash sit for 3 to 5 minutes in the uncovered pressure cooker. Remove the squash from the pressure cooker with tongs (handle gently) and serve.

Yield: 2 servings

Vegan "Pepperoni" Sausage

This seitan is an alternative to a favorite pizza topping and can be made quickly and easily in the pressure cooker. You can cut thicker slices and serve as a sausage patty with breakfast, dice up and serve in cooked beans, or even serve on crackers for an appetizer. In this recipe I suggest that you make four smaller sausages and one larger one so that you can have larger seitan cutlets for breakfast patties and smaller sausages for pepperoni slices.

FOR COOKING BROTH:

3 cups (705 ml) water

3 cups (705 ml) vegetable broth

¼ cup (60 ml) low-sodium soy sauce

FOR SEITAN:

1½ cups (180 g) vital wheat gluten

¼ cup (30 g) chickpea flour

2 tablespoons (14 g) nutritional yeast

½ teaspoon allspice

½ teaspoon paprika

½ teaspoon anise seed

½ teaspoon fennel seed, crumbled

½ teaspoon red pepper flakes

½ teaspoon garlic powder

½ teaspoon ground black pepper

1 cup (235 ml) vegetable broth, plus more as needed

1 teaspoon extra-virgin olive oil

2 tablespoons (30 ml) soy sauce

½ teaspoon vegan Worcestershire sauce

½ teaspoon liquid smoke

To make the broth: In an uncovered pressure cooker, add the broth ingredients and bring to a boil.

To make the seitan: Combine the gluten, chickpea flour, nutritional yeast, and seasonings in the bowl of a stand mixer fitted with the dough hook attachment. In a separate bowl, whisk together the broth, oil, liquid smoke, Worcestershire sauce, and liquid aminos. Add the wet ingredients to the dry ingredients and stir until well combined. Knead with the dough hook for 5 minutes.

Divided the dough in half. From one half, roll 4 small sausages and wrap individually in cheesecloth, tying the ends with string. Take the remaining half and roll into a larger sausage and wrap in cheesecloth, tying the ends with string.

Place in the boiling cooking broth, cover, and bring to pressure. Cook at pressure for 30 minutes. Allow for a natural release.

Remove the sausages from the broth to cool before handling or serving.

Yield: 8 to 10 servings

Recipe Note

If you don't have allspice, substitute a mixture of ground nutmeg, cinnamon, and cloves equal to ½ teaspoon.

CHAPTER SIX

Sauces and Dips

Pressure cooking is a great way to prepare beans and vegetables in advance and turn them into amazing additions to a meal. I love thawing beans and tossing them into the food processor for a quick, wholesome dip or to use in gravy.

Marinara Sauce, page 179

Lentil Pâté, page 179

Vegan Ranch Yogurt Dip, page 180

Asian Hot Sauce, page 181

Ginger-Cinnamon White Bean Gravy, page 182

Chickpea Hummus, page 184

Pesto-Style Bean Dip, page 186

North-Meets-South Bean Dip, page 187

Dal Dip, page 188

Spicy Red Bean Hummus, page 190

White Bean Dip, page 190

Marinara Sauce

This is a very quick sauce that

stores well in an airtight container in the refrigerator or in the freezer. You can use it with pasta, over cooked grains, or even add to soups to thicken and boost flavor.

1 teaspoon extra-virgin olive oil

4 to 6 cloves garlic, minced

1 cup (160 g) diced onion

1 teaspoon dried basil

1 teaspoon dried oregano

1 teaspoon dried parsley

1 teaspoon dried thyme

1/2 teaspoon red pepper flakes

1/4 teaspoon black pepper

1 can (28 ounces, or 784 g) crushed tomatoes

1/2 cup (120 ml) vegetable broth

1/2 teaspoon sea salt

1/2 teaspoon sugar (optional)

In an uncovered pressure cooker, heat the oil on medium-high. Add the garlic and onion and sauté for 3 minutes, until the onion is soft. Add the seasonings, tomatoes, and broth. Stir to combine.

Cover and bring to pressure. Cook at low pressure for 5 minutes. Allow for a natural release.

Remove the lid, taste, and add salt and sugar as desired.

Yield: 4 to 6 servings

Lentil Pâté

While many people think of

pâté as decidedly not vegan, there are many vegetable versions on the market and in restaurants. The lentils in this pâté add a rich color and a creamy texture. Serve with raw vegetables, pita chips, or even as a sandwich spread.

1 cup (200 g) dried lentils

2 cups (470 ml) water or vegetable broth

2 cloves garlic, minced

1 tablespoon (15 ml) lime juice

1 teaspoon sesame seeds

1/2 teaspoon sesame or extra-virgin olive oil

Add the lentils and water to the pressure cooker. Cover and bring to pressure. Cook at high pressure for 8 to 10 minutes. Allow for a natural release.

Drain the lentils, then add the lentils, lime juice, sesame seeds, and oil to a food processor. Pulse, scraping down the sides as needed, to a thick, pâté consistency.

Yield: 4 to 6 servings

Vegan Ranch Yogurt Dip

Confession: You could simply make plain vegan yogurt and add the nutritional yeast, dill, and garlic powder to make a dip. But consider this a next-level dip, for the true vegan ranch fan. The flavor in this cannot be beat. And, score, probiotic benefits from the fermenting!

2 ½ cups (588 g) shelf-stable soymilk

2 tablespoons (14 g) nutritional yeast

1 teaspoon freeze-dried dill

½ teaspoon garlic powder

½ teaspoon sugar

½ teaspoon agar powder

¼ teaspoon probiotic powder (15 million flora) or vegan starter culture

Recipe Notes

• **Alternative to shelf-stable soymilk:** Use 2 ½ cups (588 g) hot water and ¾ cup (180 ml) soymilk powder to replace the 2 ½ cups of soymilk.

• If you have probiotic capsules instead of powder, just open one and the contents should equal about the same amount of powder.

In a high-speed blender, add the soymilk, nutritional yeast, dill, garlic powder, sugar, and agar powder. Blend for 3 to 5 minutes, reaching a temperature of about 145°F (63°C) or higher.

Set aside and allow the soymilk mixture to cool down to 110°F (43°C) but not below 90°F (33°C). Note: You can speed this process up by placing the blender carafe into a bowl of ice water or by pouring the mixture into a large measuring cup and placing the covered cup in a bowl of ice water.

Once the temperature is down to 110°F (43°C), whisk the probiotic powder into the soymilk. (Don't blend it because you do not want it to heat up again.)

Pour the soymilk into two 16-ounce (470 ml) glass jars, dividing evenly, and set the uncovered jars directly into the Instant Pot. Cover the pot, move the steam release handle to sealing, and select the yogurt setting for 8 hours.

Remove the jars from the pot. Stir vigorously with a wood spoon before covering the jars with lids. Allow them to cool on the counter for an hour before storing in the refrigerator.

To serve, stir before transferring to a serving bowl.

Yield: Approximately 2½ cups of dip

Asian Hot Sauce

This is one of the few recipes I make using "pot in pot"—a method in which you put all ingredients in a dish or pan that sits on the trivet in your pressure cooker to avoid cooking directly on the liner. The main reason I use this method here is because the ingredients are highly acidic—and some quite thick—which could lead to sticking or scorching. This sauce finishes thinner than it starts by design as it's a perfect homemade alternative to store-bought hot sauce. Use this sauce for Asian-style vegan wings (page 161) instead of Buffalo sauce, as a dip for egg rolls, or pour a cup of it into a saucepan and whisk ½ teaspoon of potato starch to use as a sauce for fried or baked tofu, tempeh, or soy curls.

½ cup (120 ml) brown rice syrup

½ cup (120 ml) rice vinegar

½ cup (120 ml) mirin

¼ cup (88 g) vegan chili paste (Thai or Gochujang)

2 tablespoons (32 g) red miso

1 tablespoon (15 ml) tamari or soy sauce

1 tablespoon (8 g) sesame seeds

Add 1 cup (235 ml) of water to an uncovered Instant Pot or multicooker. Bring to a boil by using the sauté function (adjust to more heat). Set a trivet over the water.

Combine all the ingredients in glass or ceramic bowl that fits into the pot without touching the sides.

Once the water is boiling, place the bowl on the trivet. Cover the pot, move the steam release handle to sealing, select manual (high pressure), and set to 15 minutes. Once done, allow for a natural release (release after 10 minutes).

Transfer the hot sauce to a glass jar and cool at room temperature for 1 to 2 hours. Secure an airtight lid onto the jar before placing in the refrigerator. Use the sauce within 5 to 7 days.

Yield: Approximately 2 cups sauce

Ginger-Cinnamon White Bean Gravy

This protein-packed gravy is perfect to serve over mashed potatoes (page 150) and seitan (page 174). White beans, pureéd, replace the need for any type of dairy. I include this recipe in all of my holiday cooking classes because it's a student favorite.

1 cup (200 g) dried navy beans, soaked for 12 hours or overnight

1 teaspoon olive oil

3 cloves garlic, coarsely chopped

4 cups (940 ml) water

1 bay leaf

Juice of 1 lemon (about 2 tablespoons, or 30 ml)

4 tablespoons (56 g) vegan butter

½ cup (80 g) chopped yellow onion

⅛ teaspoon ground ginger

⅛ teaspoon ground cinnamon

⅛ teaspoon freshly ground black pepper

1 cup (235 ml) low-sodium vegetable broth

¼ cup (60 ml) low-sodium soy sauce

2 tablespoons (14 g) nutritional yeast (flakes or powder)

Rinse and drain the beans.

In an uncovered pressure cooker, heat the oil on medium. Add the beans, garlic, water, and bay leaf. Cover and bring to pressure. Cook at high pressure for 6 to 8 minutes. Allow for a natural release.

Remove the lid and stir in the lemon juice. Taste for doneness. If the beans are not fully cooked, simmer on low, uncovered. Set aside.

Heat the butter in a large saucepan over medium-high heat. Once the butter is melted, add the onion and sauté until translucent, 2 to 3 minutes. Add the ground ginger, cinnamon, and pepper and stir well. Stir in the broth and soy sauce. Bring to a boil. Reduce the heat and add 1½ cups (1.3 kg) of the cooked beans, using a slotted spoon. Save the remaining beans for a salad or use in the White Bean Dip (page 160).

Blend the gravy using either an immersion blender in the saucepan or transfer to a blender and pulse for 20 to 30 seconds. If using a blender, return the gravy back to the saucepan once blended.

Stir in the nutritional yeast, cover the saucepan, and cook over medium heat for 5 minutes, stirring occasionally, until slightly thickened.

Serve warm, over mashed potatoes (page 150) or root vegetables (page 151) or with a holiday roast (page 152). Leftover gravy is fantastic over seitan cutlets (page 174) or biscuits.

Yield: 3 to 4 cups (780 to 1040 g)

Chickpea Hummus

The first time I made traditional hummus in the pressure cooker

I realized there was no need to buy it from a store again. In this recipe, I add key ingredients such as onion and garlic into the cooking process itself (rather than after) and the flavors—and creamy texture—cannot be beat. I predict this will become a favorite recipe of yours too!

1 cup (200 g) dried chickpeas,
  soaked for 12 hours or overnight

1 tablespoon (15 ml) sesame oil

¹⁄₂ cup (80 g) diced yellow onion

4 or 5 cloves garlic, minced

¹⁄₂ to 1 teaspoon sea salt

¹⁄₄ cup (60 g) tahini

¹⁄₄ cup (60 ml) lemon juice

Rinse and drain the chickpeas.

In an uncovered pressure cooker, heat the oil on medium-high. Add the onion and garlic and sauté for 3 minutes, until the onion is translucent. Add the chickpeas and enough water to cover, plus another 1 inch (2.5 cm).

Cover and bring to pressure. Cook at high pressure for 13 to 15 minutes. Allow for a natural release.

Remove the lid and stir in the salt. Drain the chickpeas, reserving the cooking broth.

Add the chickpeas, tahini, and lemon juice to a food processor. Pulse to a creamy texture, adding the cooking broth as needed if the mixture is too dry. Taste and add extra salt if needed.

Yield: 4 to 6 servings

Pesto-Style Bean Dip

Traditional pesto is a sauce with garlic, basil, and pine nuts, most often blended with cheese and olive oil. There are lots of variations, and in this recipe, I went with the basic flavors and turned it into a dip that works easily in sandwiches or on salads for an entrée. Mortgage Lifters beans are a really creamy heirloom bean. If you can't find them, use butter or lima beans.

1 cup (200 g) dried Mortgage Lifter beans, soaked overnight

4 cups (940 ml) water

2 bay leaves

1 tablespoon (5 g) dried oregano

2 cloves garlic, minced

1 cup (40 g) tightly packed fresh basil leaves, chopped coarsely

1/2 cup (66 g) Brazil nuts, coarsely chopped

2 tablespoons (14 g) nutritional yeast

1/4 cup (60 ml) lemon juice

1/2 teaspoon salt

1/4 to 1/2 cup (60 to 118 ml) reserved bean broth (optional)

Rinse and drain the beans. Add beans, water, bay leaves, oregano, and garlic to the pressure cooker. Cover, heat on medium-high, and bring to pressure. Cook at high pressure for 18 to 20 minutes. Allow for a natural release.

Drain beans through a mesh strainer over a bowl to save the bean broth. Do not rinse the beans.

Transfer the beans to a food processor. Add remaining ingredients and pulse until a creamy consistency has been achieved. Use reserved bean broth if it requires more liquid.

Yield: Makes 3 cups (700 g)

North-Meets-South Bean Dip

Here's a quick and easy legume dip, featuring northern and pinto beans, perfect as a spread for veggies or crackers, as the star of a veggie sandwich wrap, or as a topper to a very veggie salad.

½ cup (100 g) dry northern beans, soaked overnight

½ cup (100 g) pinto beans, soaked overnight

2 to 3 cloves garlic, peeled and chopped coarsely

3 cups (705 ml) water or vegetable broth

2 tablespoons (30 g) tahini

2 tablespoons (30 ml) fresh lemon juice

½ teaspoon dried chili pepper

¼ cup (4 g) coarsely chopped cilantro

¼ to ½ teaspoon sea salt

1 to 2 tablespoons (15 to 30 ml) water

Rinse and drain the beans. Add the beans and enough water to cover, plus another 1 inch (2.5 cm), to the pressure cooker. Cover and bring to pressure. Cook at high pressure for 6 minutes. Allow for a natural release.

Drain the beans. Add the beans and the remaining ingredients, except the remaining water, to the food processor. Pulse quickly so that you can cream the beans but leave a few chunks (add water, as needed).

Yield: Makes 3 cups (700 g)

Dal Dip

Traditional Indian dal is a soup with red lentils. Keeping true to the spices but using less liquid, this super-healthy dip is perfect on Indian breads, such as naan or roti, as well as crackers and raw vegetables.

1 tablespoon (15 ml) sesame oil

2 cloves garlic, minced

1 cup (130 g) diced carrot

1-inch (2.5 cm) piece ginger root, minced or grated (about 2 teaspoons)

1/2 teaspoon cumin

1/2 teaspoon fennel seeds

1 cup (180 g) diced fresh tomato

1 cup (200 g) dried red lentils

2 1/4 cups (530 ml) water

2 tablespoons (30 ml) lemon juice

In an uncovered pressure cooker, heat the oil on medium-high. Add the garlic, carrot, and ginger root and sauté for 2 minutes. Add the cumin, fennel seeds, tomato, lentils, and water. Stir to combine.

Cover and bring to pressure. Cook at high pressure for 5 minutes. Allow for a natural release.

Remove the lid. Stir in the lemon juice. Transfer to a food processor or high-speed blender and pulse quickly. This should not take more than 10 seconds. Refrigerate for at least 2 hours but overnight is best. Serve cold.

Yield: 1 1/2 to 2 cups

Spicy Red Bean Hummus

Although many of us know the traditional hummus of chickpeas, tahini, and lemon juice, there are all kinds of beans and flavor profiles to play with. This one is perfect for topping crackers, dipping raw vegetables, or on a sandwich.

1 cup (200 g) dried kidney
    beans, soaked for 12 hours
    or overnight

1 seeded and diced fresh
    jalapeño

3 cloves garlic, minced

1 tablespoon (15 ml) lime juice

1 teaspoon taco seasoning

1/2 teaspoon cayenne pepper

1 tablespoon (15 ml) extra-
    virgin olive oil

1/2 teaspoon sea salt

Rinse and drain the beans.

Add the beans and enough water to cover, plus another 1 inch 2.5 cm), to the pressure cooker. Cover and bring to pressure. Cook at high pressure for 5 to 8 minutes. Allow for a natural release.

Drain the beans. Add the beans, jalapeño, garlic, lime juice, seasonings, oil, and salt to a food processor. Pulse to a creamy consistency.

Yield: 4 to 6 servings

White Bean Dip

My friend and *Vegan for Her* coauthor Ginny Messina is a big fan of simple, wholesome snacks with big flavor. This dip is inspired by her casual mention of "just puree white beans with sun-dried tomatoes."

1 cup (200 g) dried white beans,
    soaked for 12 hours or overnight

2 to 3 cups (470 to 705 ml) water or
    vegetable broth

1/2 cup (55 g) oil-packed sun-dried
    tomatoes, thinly sliced

Rinse and drain the beans.

Add the beans and enough of the water or broth to cover, plus another 1 inch (2.5 cm), to the pressure cooker. Cover and bring to pressure. Cook at high pressure for 6 to 8 minutes. Allow for a natural release.

Drain the beans. Add the beans and sun-dried tomatoes, with oil, to a food processor. Pulse to a thick purée.

Yield: 4 to 6 servings

Recipe Note

Modify this recipe by swapping out the fennel seeds and cumin with your favorite Indian spices, such as cardamom, cinnamon, coriander, garam masala, nutmeg, or saffron.

CHAPTER SEVEN

Sweet Treats

You might not think of a pressure cooker when it comes to dessert, but if you have a sweet tooth you can make most of these recipes in no time.

Coconut-Gingered Black Bean
   Brownies, page 192

Fruit and Nut Rice Pudding, page 194

Coconut Vanilla Yogurt, page 196

Easy Applesauce , page 198

Quick Fruit Jam, page 198

Banana Walnut Pudding, page 199

Peachy Butter, page 200

Coconut-Gingered Black Bean Brownies

Black bean brownies are not a new concept, but it took a while for me to fall in love with them. I decided to experiment with subtle, less "sweet" flavors—and bring my love of using my pressure cooker for homemade beans into play. These brownies are not very sweet, so consider serving them with your favorite vegan ice cream.

1½ to 2 cups (300 to 400 g) dried black beans, soaked for 12 hours or overnight

6 tablespoons (90 ml) maple, date, or brown rice syrup, divided

1 (13.5-ounce, or 378 g) can organic light coconut milk

¾ cup (184 g) no-sugar-added applesauce

2 teaspoons pure vanilla extract

1 tablespoon (8 g) freshly grated ginger or 1 teaspoon ground

½ cup (60 g) cacao powder

½ cup (60 g) millet flour (or substitute oat, quinoa, or sorghum flour)

2 tablespoons (20 g) chunks dark chocolate, chopped from a bar

¼ cup (30 g) chopped walnuts

Preheat the oven to 350°F (180°C, or gas mark 4). Line a 9 x 9-inch (23 x 23 cm) baking dish with parchment paper.

Rinse and drain the beans. Add the beans, 2 tablespoons (30 ml) of the syrup, and coconut milk to the pressure cooker. Stir to combine. Cover and bring to pressure. Cook at high pressure for 12 minutes. Allow for a natural release.

Remove the lid. If beans are not done, simmer uncovered for 5 to 10 minutes, or until cooked through.

Pour the cooked beans into a food processor fitted with an S blade and pulse to chop up the beans. Add the applesauce, vanilla, ginger, and remaining 4 tablespoons (60 ml) syrup and blend until smooth. Add the cacao powder and flour, and blend until smooth, resembling a cake batter. Add half of the dark chocolate and half of the chopped walnuts to the food processor and quickly pulse (don't blend) so the pieces are mixed in but still chunky.

Pour the batter into the prepared baking dish. Sprinkle the remaining half of the chocolate and walnut pieces on top. Bake for 40 to 50 minutes, or until a toothpick inserted into the center comes out almost clean. These brownies are fudgy, so the toothpick will still have some moist crumbs clinging to it. If necessary, bake for 5 to 10 minutes longer.

Remove the brownies and the parchment paper from the baking dish and let cool on a rack for 20 minutes. Slice into squares and serve.

Yield: 12 brownies

Fruit and Nut Rice Pudding

Back in my vegetarian days, rice pudding was my hands-down
favorite dessert. On a trip to India I saved my appetite at every meal to enjoy it. Once
vegan, I found rice pudding recipes to be a bit lacking—until I tried it in the pressure cooker!

4 tablespoons (56 g) vegan butter

1 cup (190 g) Arborio rice

3½ cups (822 ml) unsweetened
  vanilla almond milk

2 to 3 tablespoons (30 to 45 ml)
  maple, date, or brown rice
  syrup

1 teaspoon pure vanilla extract

½ teaspoon pure almond extract

¼ teaspoon ground cinnamon,
  plus more for garnish

¼ cup (35 g) golden raisins

¼ cup (35 g) chopped dried
  apricots

½ cup (55 g) slivered almonds

In an uncovered pressure cooker heat the vegan butter
on medium. Add the rice and stir to cover. Stir in the
almond milk.

Cover and bring to pressure. Cook at high pressure for
7 minutes. Use a quick release.

Remove the cover and stir in the syrup, extracts,
cinnamon, raisins, apricots, and almonds. Serve warm or
chilled with an extra sprinkle of ground cinnamon.

Yield: 6 servings

Coconut Vanilla Yogurt

To make a really thick plant-based yogurt with coconut milk, fat is
the name of the game. As in full-fat canned milk. The method with this recipe is a standard heating
method (versus the blender method on page 180). I prefer this slower heating approach to avoid
compromising the thick consistency of the milk.

2 cans (13.5 ounces, or 378 g
each) coconut milk

1 tablespoon (9 g) coconut sugar

1½ teaspoons agar powder

½ teaspoon vanilla extract

1 packet vegan culture or
¼ teaspoon probiotic powder
(15 million flora or higher), at
room temperature

Recipe Notes

- Want less tangy yogurt? Opt
for 8 to 12 hours. Like it even
tangier? Opt for 20 hours.

- My preferred brands of
coconut milk are Native
Forest Organic Milk Classic
and Thai Kitchen Coconut
Milk.

Pour two cans of coconut milk into the Instant Pot or
multicooker. Whisk in the coconut sugar. Leave the lid
off and heat the milk to 180–185°F (82–85°C) by selecting the slow cook function (adjust to less heat). Use a
thermometer to make sure that proper temperature has
been reached. Once 180°F (82°C) has been achieved,
whisk in the agar powder.

Remove the pot and pour the contents into a 4-cup
(1 L) measuring cup and allow the coconut milk to cool
to lukewarm (100–110°F [38°–43°C]). To speed the
cooling process, set the measuring cup in a bowl of cold
water; do not allow the temperature to go below 90°F
(32°C). Wash the pot liner.

Once down to 100°F (38°C), stir in the vanilla and
then add the culture packet; use a whisk to mix it with
the coconut milk until the consistency is smooth with no
lumps remaining.

Pour the yogurt into four small jam jars. Place the jars
directly in the now-clean Instant Pot (do not cover or
seal the jars). Cover the pot, move the valve to sealing,
and select the yogurt function. Increase the time to
18 hours.

When the yogurt is ready, remove the lid. Remove
the jars. You may notice a colorful film on the yogurt.
Stir it well and then seal the jars with lids. Cool at room
temperature for an hour before refrigerating. This yogurt
is best served after chilling for 8 to 24 hours.

Yield: 6 to 8 servings

Easy Applesauce

Every fall I pick up lots of apples and then think, "Uh-oh, now what do I do with them?" This applesauce is a speedy and delicious way to avoid wasting seasonal fruit. Stir it into cooked oatmeal, serve over vegan ice cream or, of course, enjoy it on it's own with a sprinkle of cinnamon.

4 cups (600 g) peeled, cored, and diced apple

2 teaspoons ground cinnamon

½ cup (120 ml) water

½ teaspoon sugar (optional)

Add the apples, cinnamon, and water to the pressure cooker. Stir to combine. Cover and bring to pressure. Cook at high pressure for 3 minutes. Use a quick release. Remove the lid. Mash the apples with a potato masher and add sugar to taste.

Yield: 4 servings

Quick Fruit Jam

My friend Justin Trollé is an elite triathlon coach and father of six. I introduced him to pressure cooking. He introduced me to this jam—a necessity, he says, when making peanut butter and jelly for his large family.

4 cups (440 g) strawberries, raspberries, or blackberries

1 cup (235 ml) water

1 cup (200 g) sugar

3 teaspoons (14 g) pectin

1 teaspoon lemon or lime juice

Add the fruit and water to the pressure cooker. Cover and bring to pressure. Cook at low pressure for 10 minutes. Use a quick release.

Remove the lid and mash the fruit with a potato masher until the fruit is broken up. Add the sugar, pectin, and lemon juice. Simmer, uncovered, stirring every couple of minutes, until the jam is tacky on the spoon, 8 to 10 minutes.

Pour through a funnel or ladle the jam into jars. Let cool before sealing with an airtight lid.

Yield: 4 cups (440 g)

Banana Walnut Pudding

When it comes to dessert, I want it fast. Another recipe that's not exactly pudding, this is a quickie nearly breadlike "pudding" with ingredients you likely have in your kitchen right now. You'll want to use four mini (3-inch or 7.5-cm) ramekins for this dessert.

2 tablespoons (28 g) vegan butter, softened

½ cup (60 g) chopped walnuts

½ teaspoon cacao powder

½ teaspoon ground cinnamon

2 small ripe bananas

¼ cup plus 1 teaspoon (65 ml) soymilk (or other plant-based milk), divided

¼ teaspoon vanilla extract

¼ teaspoon cornstarch

½ teaspoon sugar

2 tablespoons (40 g) vegan chocolate syrup or ¼ cup (44 g) vegan chocolate chips, melted, for serving (optional)

Bring 1 cup (235 ml) of water to a boil in an uncovered Instant Pot or multicooker using the sauté function (adjust to more heat). Place a trivet over the water.

In a small bowl combine the butter, walnuts, cacao powder, and cinnamon. Using four equal portions, spoon into four mini ramekins. Set side.

Peel and cut the bananas into chunks and place in a medium bowl. Add ¼ cup (60 ml) of the soymilk, the vanilla, cornstarch, and sugar. Use a potato masher to mash the ingredients. Then use a spatula to vigorously stir to a creamy texture. Add the remaining 1 teaspoon soymilk over the banana mixture and fold gently. Spoon mixture evenly over the walnut crust in each ramekin (about ¼ cup in each ramekin).

Place the ramekins on the trivet. Cover the pot, move the steam release handle to sealing, select manual, toggle the pressure button to low pressure, and set for 10 minutes. Once done, allow for a natural release (release after 10 minutes).

Use tongs or silicone gloves to remove the ramekins from the pot. Allow to cool for 15 minutes. If desired, drizzle the optional chocolate syrup or melted vegan chocolate over the pudding in each ramekin before serving.

Yield: 4 servings

Peachy Butter

This very simple recipe makes a lightly sweet spread that is terrific on fresh-baked sweet bread, such as banana bread or even on oats for breakfast. For dessert drizzle it over vegan ice cream. In addition to being simple and delicious, peaches are a good source of vitamin C.

3 cups (510 g) diced peaches

1 cup (235 ml) water

1 teaspoon ground cinnamon

1 teaspoon vegan butter

Add the peaches, water, and cinnamon to the pressure cooker. Cover and bring to pressure. Cook at high pressure for 3 minutes. Use a quick release method.

Remove the cover and mash the peaches with a potato masher. Add the vegan butter and simmer on low, uncovered, for 2 to 3 minutes to cook down any excess liquid; it should have a thick, jam-like consistency.

Yield: 2 cups (500 g)

Recipe Note

Nectarines are a great substitute for peaches, or consider a combination of both.

Resources

Recommended Pressure Cookers

STOVETOP
Fagor Chef Pressure Cooker (It's expensive, but I love it!)
Fagor 2-by-1 Splendid 5-Piece Pressure Cooker Set
Presto 4-Quart (3.8 L) Stainless Steel Pressure Cooker
Presto 01365 6-Quart (5.8 L) Stainless Steel Pressure Cooker, Deluxe
Presto 307912 6-Quart (5.8 L) Stainless Steel Pressure Cooker

ELECTRIC
Instant Pot 7 In 1 Multi-Use Programmable Pressure Cooker
Fagor LUX Electric Multicooker
GoWISE GW22620 8-in-1 Electric Pressure Cooker

Recommended Websites

www.jlgoesvegan.com
www.hippressurecooking.com
www.facebook.com/groups/veganpressurecooking

Recommended Classes

Author JL Fields offers pressure cooking and other culinary classes in Colorado Springs, Colorado and the surrounding area. She teaches private online cooking lessons via video platform for anyone outside of the Colorado Spirngs area. Visit CSVeganCooking.com to learn more.

Acknowledgments

It was a privilege to work with the enthusiastic and encouraging team at Fair Winds Press. Special thanks to Amanda Waddell for being a thoughtful and patient editor, and to project manager Betsy Gammons, art director Heather Godin, book designer Amanda Richmond, and publisher Winnie Prentiss. Thank you for putting great vegan content out into the world.

Brilliantly talented Kate Lewis, thank you for turning my recipes into works of art through your photos.

Heartfelt thanks to my agent Angela Miller, who inherited me on a previous project and kept me for this, and future projects. I am grateful for your support and encouragement.

My recipe testers—several of whom had never touched a pressure cooker prior to this project—are my heroes! My thanks to Ashley Flitter, Barb Musick, Barbara Ravid, Ben Covington, Bonnie Hildebrand, Carolina Meyer, Cat DiStasio, Connie Maschan, Jared Bigman, Kathleen Graas, Kavitha Selvaraj, Lauren Collier, Laurie Morrison, Linda Lauder, Lisa Poveda, Liz Dee, Marcia Kalisch, Marti Miller Hall, Melissa McPherson, Shannon Kinsella, Vegan Mos (Michael Suchman and Ethan Ciment), Wendy Moniuk, and Whitney Ferdon.

Ginny Messina and Victoria Moran: I can never thank you enough for walking beside me as friends, mentors, and colleagues. Thank you for your unwavering commitment to the animals.

I am privileged to lead the Colorado Springs Vegan & Vegetarian Group and am so incredibly thankful to each and every member for embracing me when I became a Coloradan.

I am humbled and devoted to my blog readers. Always.

Mom, dad, and my sisters—thank you for never being surprised by what I do.

To my husband Dave, thank you for being my biggest supporter, for being open to a veg journey, and for being the best cat daddy ever to CK and Ernie.

Going vegan changed my life. I wish for a world free of harm and cruelty to every single being. That's why I create vegan recipes—for the animals.

About the Author

JL Fields is an author, culinary instructor, columnist, speaker, activist, and radio personality. She is the founder and director of the Colorado Springs Vegan Cooking Academy, the author of *The Vegan Air Fryer*, *Vegan Pressure Cooking*, and coauthor of *The Main Street Vegan Academy Cookbook* and *Vegan for Her*. The publisher of JL Goes Vegan.com, JL has received culinary training at the Natural Gourmet Institute and the Christina Pirello School of Natural Cooking and Integrative Health Studies. She teaches vegan cooking in the culinary arts program at the University of New Mexico at Taos. She is a Main Street Vegan Academy–certified Vegan Lifestyle Coach and Educator and a certified Food for Life instructor with Physicians Committee for Responsible Medicine (PCRM). She writes and broadcasts from Colorado Springs, Colorado.

About the Photographer

Kate Lewis is a New York City– and Ohio–based food and travel photographer and stylist. Over the years, she has held every restaurant position from hostess, server, and bartender to chocolatier, barista, and chef. Her culinary background and fine art training combined with her passion for food prompted her to begin shooting portraits for renowned chefs and highly-stylized photographs. Kate's photography and styling has worked with national publications like *Food & Wine*, *VegNews*, and more than ten cookbooks. Follow Kate's everyday adventures on Instagram and Twitter @_Kate_Lewis.

Index

Acorn Squash, Seitan-Stuffed, 175
adzuki beans
    Asian Adzuki Bean Chili, 100
    Gingered Adzuki Beans, Greens, and
        Grains, 111
    Three Bean Delight, 30
almond milk
    Apple Pie Steel-Cut Oats, 56
    Fruit and Nut Rice Pudding, 195
    Potato Soup, 70
almonds
    Almond Garlic Green Beans, 135
    Fruit and Nut Rice Pudding, 195
    Savory Oat Porridge, 58
amaranth
    Amaranth Lentils, 110
    Oat, Amaranth, and Carrot
        Porridge, 61
    Pumpkin Spice Porridge, 59
    Savory Oat Porridge, 58
anasazi beans
    Anasazi Bean and Potato Soup, 86
    Umami Anasazi Beans, 27
apples
    Apple Pie Steel-Cut Oats, 56
    Basic Vegetable Broth, 63
    Easy Applesauce, 198
    Flageolet Bean and Millet Stew, 91
    Potato, Apple, and Lentil Soup, 79
Arborio rice
    Fava Bean Risotto, 120
    Fruit and Nut Rice Pudding, 195
    Lemon Green Bean Risotto, 38
artichokes
    Lemony Artichokes with Horseradish
        Butter, 136
    Tofu, Chickpea, Artichoke, and Potato
        Soup, 80
arugula
    Mediterranean Beans with Greens, 172
    White Beans and Greens Soup, 66
Asian Adzuki Bean Chili, 100
Asian Hot Sauce, 181
Asparagus and Potato Soup, Cream of, 84
Ayocote Morado beans, 113

"Bacon" and Cabbage, Vegan, 114
"Baked" Sweet Potatoes, 143
Balsamic Black Beans, 28
Banana Walnut Pudding, 199
barley
    Basic Pearl Barley, 47
    Bean and Barley Stew, 81
    Italian Pearl Barley, 47
    Korean Kongbap, 117

Lentil, Kale, and Barley Risotto, 118
Mediterranean Beans with Greens, 172
Portobello Mushroom and Barley
    Soup, 77
Split Pea and Barley Stew, 92
basil: Pesto-Style Bean Dip, 186
Bean and Barley Stew, 81
beans. See also specific types
    Bean and Barley Stew, 81
    Breakfast (or not) Bean & Potato
        Hash, 113
    cooking time, 10, 19
    North-Meets-South Bean Dip, 187
    Speedy Bean Chili, 87
    tips for cooking, 23
    Vegan "Turkey," Bean, and Kale
        Soup, 82
beets
    cooking time, 18
    Flageolet Bean and Millet Stew, 91
black beans
    Balsamic Black Beans, 28
    Black Bean and Sweet Potato Stew, 89
    Black Beans and Quinoa, 104
    Black Beans and Yams, 111
    Coconut-Gingered Black Bean
        Brownies, 192
    Easy Black Bean Soup, 65
blackberries: Quick Fruit Jam, 198
black-eyed peas
    Black-Eyed Pea and Collard Green
        Chili, 99
    Black-Eyed Peas and Farro, 121
    Quick-and-Easy Rice and Peas, 112
bok choy
    Bok Choy, Mushrooms, and Onion
        with Tamari Lime Dressing, 138
    White Beans and Greens Soup, 66
Brazil nuts: Pesto-Style Bean Dip, 186
breakfasts
    Apple Pie Steel Cut Oats, 56
    Breakfast (or not) Bean & Potato
        Hash, 113
    Brown Rice and Farro Porridge, 55
    Cheesy Spinach Oats, 52
    Couscous, Oatmeal, and Veggie
        Porridge, 53
    Multigrain and TVP Hot Cereal, 58
    Oat, Amaranth, and Carrot
        Porridge, 61
    Pumpkin Spice Porridge, 59
    Savory Oat Porridge, 58
Broccoli Bowl, Polenta, 45
broth
    Basic Vegetable Broth, 63

Vegetable Scrap Broth, 64
Brownies, Coconut-Gingered Black
    Bean, 192
brown rice
    Brown Rice, 33
    Brown Rice and Farro Porridge, 55
    Gingered Adzuki Beans, Greens, and
        Grains, 111
    Korean Kongbap, 117
    Mint Chive Brown Rice, 37
    Mushroom Rice, 34
    Spanish Rice, 37
Brussels Sprouts, Rosemary and
    Thyme, 132
buckwheat, 19
Buffalo Sauce, 161–162
Bulgur Paprika, 48
bulk cooking, 22
Butter, Peachy, 200
butternut squash: Kale, Lentil, and Squash
    Chili, 90

cabbage
    Asian Adzuki Bean Chili, 100
    Vegan "Bacon" and Cabbage, 114
cannellini beans
    Mediterranean Beans with Greens, 172
    White Beans and Greens Soup, 66
carrots
    Asian Adzuki Bean Chili, 100
    Basic Vegetable Broth, 63
    Black Bean and Sweet Potato Stew, 89
    Black Beans and Quinoa, 104
    Black-Eyed Pea and Collard Green
        Chili, 99
    Chik'n Lentil Noodle Soup, 74
    Chunky Red Lentil Stew, 96
    Couscous, Oatmeal, and Veggie
        Porridge, 53
    Creamy Kale Miso Soup, 73
    Curried Mung Bean Stew, 69
    Dal Dip, 188
    Easy Black Bean Soup, 65
    Garam Masala Lentil Soup, 65
    Holiday Roast with Mashed
        Vegetables, 152
    Instant Pot Miso Soup, 85
    Italian Soybean Balls and Tomato
        Sauce, 166–167
    New World Székely Goulash, 107
    Oat, Amaranth, and Carrot
        Porridge, 61
    Portobello Mushroom and Barley
        Soup, 77
    Potato, Apple, and Lentil Soup, 79

Potato Soup, 70
Quick-and-Easy Rice and Peas, 112
Quinoa Pilaf, 42
Root Veggie Tagine, 141
Savory Root Vegetable Mash, 151
Shepherd's Pie, 149
Speedy Bean Chili, 87
Split Pea and Barley Stew, 92
Tofu Scramble, 130
Vegan "Turkey," Bean, and Kale
    Soup, 82
White Beans and Greens Soup, 66
cauliflower, 18
Cheesy Spinach Oats, 52
chickpeas
    Chickpea Hummus, 185
    Cinnamon-Curried Chickpeas, 25
    New World Székely Goulash, 107
    Tofu, Chickpea, Artichoke, and Potato
        Soup, 80
Chik'n Lentil Noodle Soup, 74
chili
    Asian Adzuki Bean Chili, 100
    Black-Eyed Pea and Collard Green
        Chili, 99
    Chili-Style Kidney Beans, 29
    Kale, Lentil, and Squash Chili, 90
    Speedy Bean Chili, 87
    Summer Lentil and Millet Chili, 102
chocolate: Coconut-Gingered Black Bean
    Brownies, 192
Cinnamon-Curried Chickpeas, 25
coconut milk
    Coconut-Gingered Black Bean
        Brownies, 192
    Coconut Vanilla Yogurt, 196
    Pumpkin Spice Porridge, 59
    Sweet Red Lentil Coconut Curry, 127
collard greens
    Black-Eyed Pea and Collard Green
        Chili, 99
    Curried Mung Bean Stew, 69
    Gingered Adzuki Beans, Greens, and
        Grains, 111
    White Beans and Greens Soup, 66
cooking time charts, 18–19
corn
    Brown Rice and Farro Porridge, 55
    Fiesta Soy Curl and Rice
        Casserole, 169
    Instant Pot Miso Soup, 85
    Speedy Bean Chili, 87
couscous
    Couscous, Oatmeal, and Veggie
        Porridge, 53
    Pumpkin Spice Porridge, 59
Cranberries, Wild Rice with Dried
    Cherries and, 48
Cream of Asparagus and Potato Soup, 84
Creamy Kale Miso Soup, 73
curries
    Cinnamon-Curried Chickpeas, 25
    Curried Mung Bean Stew, 69

Sweet Red Lentil Coconut Curry, 127

Dal Dip, 188
Dill Long-Grain White Rice, 33
dips
    Chickpea Hummus, 185
    Dal Dip, 188
    Lentil Pâté, 179
    North-Meets-South Bean Dip, 187
    Pesto-Style Bean Dip, 186
    Spicy Red Bean Hummus, 190
    Vegan Ranch Yogurt Dip, 180
    White Bean Dip, 190
Dressing, Tamari Lime, 138
dulse flakes
    Asian Adzuki Bean Chili, 100
    Three Bean Delight, 30

electric pressure cookers, 12, 15
elevation, 14
Enchiladas, Jackfruit and Sweet
    Potato, 163
escarole, 18

Fagor LUX multicooker, 17
farro
    Black-Eyed Peas and Farro, 121
    Brown Rice and Farro Porridge, 55
Fava Bean Risotto, 120
Flageolet Bean and Millet Stew, 91
foaming, beans and grains, 12–13
freekeh
    Freekeh, 40
    Turnips and Tomatoes over
        Freekeh, 133
fruit. See also specific types
    Fruit and Nut Rice Pudding, 195
    Quick Fruit Jam, 198

Garam Masala Lentil Soup, 65
garbanzo beans. See chickpeas
Garlicky Kale and Potatoes, 145
Ginger-Cinnamon White Bean Gravy, 182
Gingered Adzuki Beans, Greens, and
    Grains, 111
GoWISE multicooker, 17
grains. See also specific types
    about, 32
    breakfast, 51
    cooking time, 19
Gravy, Ginger-Cinnamon White Bean, 182
Great Northern beans
    North-Meets-South Bean Dip, 187
    Vegan "Turkey," Bean, and Kale Soup,
        82
green beans
    Almond Garlic Green Beans, 135
    Bean and Barley Stew, 81
    Chik'n Lentil Noodle Soup, 74
greens. See also specific types
    Gingered Adzuki Beans, Greens, and
        Grains, 111
    Mediterranean Beans with Greens, 172

Navy Beans, Rice, and Greens, 105
White Beans and Greens Soup, 66

herbamare, 30
hippie bowl, 22
Holiday Roast with Mashed
    Vegetables, 152
hummus
    Chickpea Hummus, 185
    Spicy Red Bean Hummus, 190

Instant Pot, 15–17
Italian Lentils, 24
Italian Pearl Barley, 47
Italian Soybean Balls and Tomato Sauce,
    166–167

jackfruit
    Jackfruit and Sweet Potato
        Enchiladas, 163
    Pulled Jackfruit Sandwiches, 156
jalapeño peppers
    Anasazi Bean and Potato Soup, 86
    Bean and Barley Stew, 81
    Black-Eyed Pea and Collard Green
        Chili, 99
    Lentil, Kale, and Barley Risotto, 118
    Pinquito Bean Burger, 157–158
    Refried Bean and Tempeh Soup
        (or Stew), 95
    Refried Beans, 170
    Spicy Red Bean Hummus, 190
    Summer Lentil and Millet Chili, 102
    Tempeh Tacos or Tostadas, 164
Jam, Quick Fruit, 198

Kabocha Squash, Steamed, 137
kale
    Creamy Kale Miso Soup, 73
    Garlicky Kale and Potatoes, 145
    Gingered Adzuki Beans, Greens, and
        Grains, 111
    Kale, Lentil, and Squash Chili, 90
    Lentil, Kale, and Barley Risotto, 118
    Navy Beans, Rice, and Greens, 105
    Shepherd's Pie, 149
    Summer Lentil and Millet Chili, 102
    Tofu Scramble, 130
    Vegan "Turkey," Bean, and Kale
        Soup, 82
    White Beans and Greens Soup, 66
kidney beans
    Chili-Style Kidney Beans, 29
    Speedy Bean Chili, 87
    Spicy Red Bean Hummus, 190
    Three Bean Delight, 30
kombu
    Gingered Adzuki Beans, Greens, and
        Grains, 111
    Three Bean Delight, 30
Korean Kongbap, 117

Lemon Green Bean Risotto, 38
Lemony Artichokes with Horseradish
    Butter, 136
lentils
    Amaranth Lentils, 110
    Chik'n Lentil Noodle Soup, 74
    Chunky Red Lentil Stew, 96
    cooking time, 10, 19
    Dal Dip, 188
    Garam Masala Lentil Soup, 65
    Italian Lentils, 24
    Kale, Lentil, and Squash Chili, 90
    Lentil, Kale, and Barley Risotto, 118
    Lentil Pâté, 179
    Lentil TVP Taco Meat, 50
    Potato, Apple, and Lentil Soup, 79
    Shepherd's Pie, 149
    Summer Lentil and Millet Chili, 102
lima beans, 19

mac 'n cheese
    Soy Curl Mac 'n Cheese, 123
    Taco Mac 'n Cheese, 124
Marinara Sauce, 179
Mediterranean Beans with Greens, 172
millet
    Quinoa-Millet-Pea Bowl, 108
    Summer Lentil and Millet Chili, 102
miso
    Creamy Kale Miso Soup, 73
    Instant Pot Miso Soup, 85
money savings, 11
Mortgage Lifter beans, 186
multicooker, 15–17
Multigrain and TVP Hot Cereal, 58
Mung Bean Stew, Curried, 69
mushrooms
    Bean and Barley Stew, 81
    Bok Choy, Mushrooms, and Onion
        with Tamari Lime Dressing, 138
    Fava Bean Risotto, 120
    Gingered Adzuki Beans, Greens, and
        Grains, 111
    Mushroom Rice, 34
    Portobello Mushroom and Barley
        Soup, 77
    Potato Soup, 70
    Seitan-Stuffed Acorn Squash, 175
    Split Pea and Barley Stew, 92
    Tempeh Tacos or Tostadas, 164
    Vegan "Loose Meat" Sandwiches, 155
    White Beans and Greens Soup, 66

natural pressure release (NPR), 14
navy beans
    Bean and Barley Stew, 81
    Ginger-Cinnamon White Bean Gravy,
        182
    Mediterranean Beans with Greens, 172
    Navy Beans, Rice, and Greens, 105
    White Beans and Rice, 171
New World Székely Goulash, 107
normal release, 14

oats
    Apple Pie Steel-Cut Oats, 56
    Cheesy Spinach Oats, 52
    cooking time, 19
    Couscous, Oatmeal, and Veggie
        Porridge, 53
    Oat, Amaranth, and Carrot
        Porridge, 61
    Savory Oat Porridge, 58
oil, 13
okra, 18
onions, 18

parsnips: Flageolet Bean and Millet
    Stew, 91
peaches
    Basic Vegetable Broth, 63
    Peachy Butter, 200
peas
    Korean Kongbap, 117
    Mashed Peas and Potatoes, 146
    Quinoa-Millet-Pea Bowl, 108
    Split Pea and Barley Stew, 92
    Very Veggie Split Pea Soup, 78
pepperoni, vegan: White Beans and
    Rice, 171
peppers. See also jalapeño peppers
    Breakfast (or not) Bean & Potato
        Hash, 113
    Instant POT-ato Salad, 143
    Italian Soybean Balls and Tomato
        Sauce, 166–167
    Kale, Lentil, and Squash Chili, 90
    Speedy Bean Chili, 87
    Taco Mac 'n Cheese, 124
Pesto-Style Bean Dip, 186
Pinquito Bean Burger, 157–158
pinto beans
    North-Meets-South Bean Dip, 187
    Refried Bean and Tempeh Soup
        (or Stew), 95
    Refried Beans, 170
    Three Bean Delight, 30
plums, umeboshi, 111
polenta, Polenta Broccoli Bowl, 45
porridge
    Oat, Amaranth, and Carrot Porridge,
        61
    Pumpkin Spice Porridge, 59
    Savory Oat Porridge, 58
Portobello Mushroom and Barley Soup, 77
potatoes
    Anasazi Bean and Potato Soup, 86
    Breakfast (or not) Bean & Potato
        Hash, 113
    Cream of Asparagus and Potato
        Soup, 84
    Garlicky Kale and Potatoes, 145
    Holiday Roast with Mashed
        Vegetables, 152
    Instant POT-ato Salad, 143
    Mashed Peas and Potatoes, 146
    Potato, Apple, and Lentil Soup, 79

Potato Soup, 70
    Savory Root Vegetable Mash, 151
    Shepherd's Pie, 149
    Split Pea and Barley Stew, 92
    Tofu, Chickpea, Artichoke, and Potato
        Soup, 80
    Vegan "Bacon" and Cabbage, 114
pressure cookers
    care of, 20
    electric and stove top, 15
    purchasing, 15
    sizes of, 15
    tips and tricks, 20
pressure cooking
    advantages of, 10–11
    electric vs. gas stove, 17
puddings
    Banana Walnut Pudding, 199
    Fruit and Nut Rice Pudding, 195
Pumpkin Spice Porridge, 59

quick release, 14
quinoa
    Basic Quinoa, 41
    Black Beans and Quinoa, 104
    Pumpkin Spice Porridge, 59
    Quinoa-Millet-Pea Bowl, 108
    Quinoa Pilaf, 42

raspberries: Quick Fruit Jam, 198
Refried Bean and Tempeh Soup (or Stew),
    95
Refried Beans, 170
resources, pressure cooking, 202
rice
    Brown Rice, 33
    Brown Rice and Farro Porridge, 55
    cooking time, 19
    Dill Long-Grain White Rice, 32
    Fava Bean Risotto, 120
    Fiesta Soy Curl and Rice
        Casserole, 169
    Fruit and Nut Rice Pudding, 195
    Gingered Adzuki Beans, Greens, and
        Grains, 111
    Korean Kongbap, 117
    Lemon Green Bean Risotto, 38
    Mint Chive Brown Rice, 37
    Mushroom Rice, 34
    Navy Beans, Rice, and Greens, 105
    Quick-and-Easy Rice and Peas, 112
    Spanish Rice, 37
    Sweet Red Lentil Coconut Curry, 127
    White Beans and Rice, 171
    Wild Rice with Dried Cherries and
        Cranberries, 48
risotto
    Fava Bean Risotto, 120
    Lemon Green Bean Risotto, 38
    Lentil, Kale, and Barley Risotto, 118
Root Veggie Tagine, 141
Rosemary and Thyme Brussels
    Sprouts, 132

safety precautions, 12
saffron
    Root Veggie Tagine, 141
    Very Veggie Split Pea Soup, 78
salt, 20
sandwiches
    Pulled Jackfruit Sandwiches, 156
    Vegan "Loose Meat" Sandwiches, 155
sauces
    Asian Hot Sauce, 181
    Buffalo Sauce, 161–162
    Ginger-Cinnamon White Bean Gravy,
        182
    Italian Soybean Balls and Tomato
        Sauce, 166–167
    Marinara Sauce, 179
sauerkraut: New World Székely Goulash,
    107
seitan
    Basic Seitan, 174
    Seitan-Stuffed Acorn Squash, 175
    Seitan Swiss Steak, 128
    Vegan Buffalo Wings, 161–162
    Vegan "Pepperoni" Sausage, 177
Shepherd's Pie, 149
soaking beans, 23
soba noodles: Chik'n Lentil Noodle Soup,
    74
soups and stews. See also broth; chili
    Anasazi Bean and Potato Soup, 86
    Basic Vegetable Broth, 63
    Bean and Barley Stew, 81
    Black Bean and Sweet Potato Stew, 89
    Chik'n Lentil Noodle Soup, 74
    Chunky Red Lentil Stew, 96
    Cream of Asparagus and Potato
        Soup, 84
    Creamy Kale Miso Soup, 73
    Curried Mung Bean Stew, 69
    Easy Black Bean Soup, 65
    Flageolet Bean and Millet Stew, 91
    Garam Masala Lentil Soup, 65
    Instant Pot Miso Soup, 85
    Portobello Mushroom and Barley
        Soup, 77
    Potato, Apple, and Lentil Soup, 79
    Potato Soup, 70
    Refried Bean and Tempeh Soup
        (or Stew), 95
    Root Veggie Tagine, 141
    Split Pea and Barley Stew, 92
    Tofu, Chickpea, Artichoke, and Potato
        Soup, 80
    Vegan "Turkey," Bean, and Kale
        Soup, 82
    Very Veggie Split Pea Soup, 78
    White Beans and Greens Soup, 66
soybeans
    Italian Soybean Balls and Tomato
        Sauce, 166–167
    Korean Kongbap, 117

soy curls
    Fiesta Soy Curl and Rice Casserole,
        169
    Soy Curl Mac 'n Cheese, 123
Spanish Rice, 37
Speedy Bean Chili, 87
spelt berries: Pinquito Bean Burger,
    157–158
Spicy Red Bean Hummus, 190
spinach
    Cheesy Spinach Oats, 52
    Tempeh Tacos or Tostadas, 164
    White Beans and Greens Soup, 66
split peas
    Split Pea and Barley Stew, 92
    Very Veggie Split Pea Soup, 78
squash
    cooking time, 18
    Kale, Lentil, and Squash Chili, 90
    Seitan-Stuffed Acorn Squash, 175
    Steamed Kabocha Squash, 137
    Summer Lentil and Millet Chili, 102
stews. See soups and stews
strawberries: Quick Fruit Jam, 198
sushi rice: Sweet Red Lentil Coconut
    Curry, 127
sweet potatoes
    "Baked" Sweet Potatoes, 143
    Black Bean and Sweet Potato Stew, 89
    Curried Mung Bean Stew, 69
    Jackfruit and Sweet Potato Enchiladas,
        163
    Mashed Sweet Potatoes, 150
    Root Veggie Tagine, 141
    Sweet Red Lentil Coconut Curry, 127
Swiss chard
    Amaranth Lentils, 110
    Gingered Adzuki Beans, Greens, and
        Grains, 111
    White Beans and Greens Soup, 66

tacos
    Taco Mac 'n Cheese, 124
    Tempeh Tacos or Tostadas, 164
tahini
    Chickpea Hummus, 185
    North-Meets-South Bean Dip, 187
tempeh
    Refried Bean and Tempeh Soup
        (or Stew), 95
    Tempeh Tacos or Tostadas, 164
Three Bean Delight, 30
tofu
    Cream of Asparagus and Potato Soup,
        84
    Creamy Kale Miso Soup, 73
    Instant Pot Miso Soup, 85
    Potato Soup, 70
    Tofu, Chickpea, Artichoke, and Potato
        Soup, 80
    Tofu Scramble, 130

tomatoes
    Instant POT-ato Salad, 143
    Mediterranean Beans with Greens, 172
    Taco Mac 'n Cheese, 124
    Tomato Sauce, Italian Soybean Balls
        and, 166–167
    Turnips and Tomatoes over
        Freekeh, 133
    Veggie Stewed Tomatoes, 142
    White Bean Dip, 190
Tostadas, Tempeh Tacos or, 164
turnips
    Root Veggie Tagine, 141
    Savory Root Vegetable Mash, 151
    Turnips and Tomatoes over
        Freekeh, 133
TVP (textured vegetable protein)
    Italian Soybean Balls and Tomato
        Sauce, 166–167
    Lentil TVP Taco Meat, 50
    Multigrain and TVP Hot Cereal, 58
    Taco Mac 'n Cheese, 124
    Vegan "Loose Meat" Sandwiches, 155
    Vegan "Turkey," Bean, and Kale
        Soup, 82

Umami Anasazi Beans, 27

Vegan "Bacon" and Cabbage, 114
Vegan Buffalo Wings, 161–162
Vegan "Loose Meat" Sandwiches, 155
Vegan "Pepperoni" Sausage, 177
Vegan Ranch Yogurt Dip, 180
Vegan "Turkey," Bean, and Kale Soup, 82
vegetables. See also specific types
    cooking time for, 18
    Couscous, Oatmeal, and Veggie
        Porridge, 53
    Root Veggie Tagine, 141
    Savory Root Vegetable Mash, 151
    Vegetable Scrap Broth, 64
    Veggie Stewed Tomatoes, 142
    Very Veggie Split Pea Soup, 78

Walnut Pudding, Banana, 199
white beans
    Ginger-Cinnamon White Bean Gravy,
        182
    White Bean Dip, 190
    White Beans and Greens Soup, 66
    White Beans and Rice, 171
Wild Rice with Dried Cherries and
    Cranberries, 48

Yams, Black Beans and, 111
yogurt
    Coconut Vanilla Yogurt, 196
    Vegan Ranch Yogurt Dip, 180

zucchini: Quinoa-Millet-Pea Bowl, 108

CPSIA information can be obtained
at www.ICGtesting.com
Printed in the USA
LVHW021434290319
612201LV00006BA/6/P